French Braid Quilts

*14 Quick Quilts
with Dramatic Results*

Jane Hardy Miller

C&T PUBLISHING

Text © 2006 Jane Hardy Miller

Artwork © 2006 C&T Publishing

Publisher: Amy Marson

Editorial Director: Gailen Runge

Acquisitions Editor: Jan Grigsby

Editor: Liz Aneloski

Technical Editors: Carolyn Aune, Robyn Gronning

Copyeditor/Proofreader: Wordfirm, Inc.

Cover Designer/Design Director/Book Designer:
   Kristy K. Zacharias

Illustrator: Tim Manibusan

Production Assistant: Kerry Graham

Photography: Luke Mulks and Diane Pedersen, unless
   otherwise noted

Published by C&T Publishing, Inc., P.O. Box 1456,
   Lafayette, CA 94549

Front cover: Shadow City

Back cover: Lucy's Leftover Watercolor Kit and Thanks, Frank

Library of Congress Cataloging-in-Publication Data

Miller, Jane Hardy

   French braid quilts : 14 quick quilts with dramatic results / Jane
Hardy Miller.

   p. cm.

   Includes index.

   ISBN 1-57120-326-5 (paper trade)

   1. Quilting—Patterns. I. Title.

TT835.M515 2006

746.46'041—dc22

2005017282

Printed in China

10 9 8 7 6 5 4 3 2 1

Contents

Acknowledgments/Dedication 4

Introduction 5

1 Chapter One
Equipment 6

   Anatomy of a French Braid 7

2 Chapter Two
Fabric Selection 8

   Braid-Run Fabrics 8

   Accent Fabric 10

   Triangle Fabrics 10

   Separator-Band Fabrics 12

   Border Fabrics 12

3 Chapter Three
Basic French Braid Construction 13

   Cutting the Braid-Run Fabrics 13

   Cutting the Starting Triangles 14

   Laying Out the Braid .14

   Troubleshooting 15

   Cutting the Accent Fabric 15

   Cutting the Ending Triangles 15

   Sewing the Braids 16

   Trimming Braids Without Separator Bands 17

Sewing Braids Together 19

Project 1: Lucy's Leftover Watercolor Kit 20

Project 2: Formal Affair .22

4 Chapter Four
Adding Basic Separator Bands 25

Marking the Braids 25

Cutting the Separator Bands 26

Getting It All Together 26

Project 3: Cornucopia 28

Project 4: Passion for Purple 30

Project 5: Baby Braid 32

5 Chapter Five
Braid Variations 34

Center-Out French Braids 34

Project 6: Oriental Palms 36

End-In French Braids 38

Project 7: It's Always Green in Miami 40

Project 8: Thanks, Frank 42

Project 9: Mi Casa Es Su Casa 45

6 Chapter Six
Adding Separator Band Variations 49

Simple Pieced Separator Bands 49

Project 10: Lava Lamp 50

French Braids as Separator Bands 52

Project 11: Shadow City 54

Separators Using Reverse Braid Order 57

Project 12: Big Red .58

Separator Bands that Align with the Braids 61

Reconstructed French Braids as Separator Bands   61

Project 13: Café Ole .64

Chevron Separator Braids 66

Project 14: Am I Blue? 68

7 Chapter Seven
Adjusting the Size 70

Adjusting the Width 70

Adjusting the Length 70

Using the Tables 70

8 Chapter Eight
Finishing 72

9 Chapter Nine
Quilting Basics 73

Butted Borders 73

Backing 73

Batting 73

Layering 73

Basting 73

Binding 74

Appendix: Yardage and Cutting Charts   75

About the Authors 79

Acknowledgments

So many people helped me with this book that it should be considered a joint effort, and I very much appreciate their help and forbearance. "Fabulous Florals," a Plumples quilt pattern by Arlene Netten, served as the inspiration and starting point for the quilts. Stephanie Cohen gave me an enormous amount of her time and support, did photography and photo printing on request, made several quilt labels, and provided in-home computer technical support. Joan Bailey McMath proofread numerous versions of the book; she also loaned me her camera at several crucial points, then talked me down when I couldn't make it work. These two women alternated in the dispensing of pep talks. Brian Partin invented the name "French braid," which gave a whole new feel to a traditional pattern; named several of the quilts; and graciously pretended that he didn't mind climbing up the big ladder to display them. Lucy Mansfield was the person who talked me into making the quilts into a book. Some days I thanked her, and some days I just rolled my eyes! Eddie Mansfield kept my sewing machines running perfectly, an endless but not thankless task. My co-workers, Edith Matthews and Lynn Kern, were nice to me even when the only words that came out of my mouth, for months on end, were "French" and "braid." Many of my students allowed me to use them as experimental subjects, but Lois Willoughby became addicted to French braid quilts and generously loaned me one for use in this book. And the entire quilting community in Miami has been consistently encouraging and supportive. Thank you all so much. I couldn't have done it without you.

Dedication

This book is dedicated to Frances Hardy, who taught me how to sew, and to Irving Miller, who always said I should write a book. They both thought I could do anything.

Introduction

You are probably familiar with log cabin quilts. Quilters love them for their simplicity of pattern, ease of piecing, and versatility in setting—you can do a lot with something that's easy to make. You might also know a variation, the log cabin with cornerstones—squares are pieced into the corners where the "logs" intersect. French braid quilts combine these techniques. They are strippie, two-sided log cabins with cornerstones.

If at this point you have decided that this type of quilt is way too complicated, keep reading anyway. My students have found French braids to be among the easiest and quickest of quilts to construct. Most of the cutting and sewing involves strips and rectangles, so there aren't any triangle corners to align (or to separate as they approach the needle). Forget eighths and sixteenths of an inch—the smallest measurement you'll use is a quarter inch.

These quilts are also extremely forgiving, with a high tolerance for minor errors and personal differences in seam allowances, and the results are dramatic, whether your fabric selection tends toward calm and peaceful or knockout. French braids also give you a lot of quilt for your sewing time. Although they look complicated, the quilts are simple to piece, and once you've learned the techniques, the variations are endless.

To help you plan, I've included an appendix that will teach you how to change the size of the quilt; it also includes additional yardage charts and cutting charts.

For many of my students, French braid quilts are extremely addictive—most people make at least two, and four or five is not uncommon. I hope you have as much fun with this design as I have.

1 Equipment

Your sewing machine is the item that most affects the quality of your quilting, so buy the best you can afford and become familiar with it. Tension problems and poor stitch quality will result in a final product that is less than satisfactory, so be sure to clean and oil your machine frequently. And no matter how infrequently you use it, have it serviced regularly.

Before beginning a project, replace the sewing machine needle with a new one. I use a Schmetz size 70/10 Jeans or Microtex needle. Both types are sharper than the standard Universal needles and penetrate the fibers more accurately; I prefer the smaller size for the same reason.

The only other required sewing machine accessory is some kind of mechanism to maintain a ¼″ seam allowance—I prefer a ¼″-seam presser foot. When you get to the point of quilting the layers, you may also want a walking foot or a free-motion quilting foot; generic models of all these feet can be purchased if they are not available for your model of sewing machine.

You will need a rotary cutter and a cutting mat. Most quilters have a favorite brand of rotary cutter. Because rotary cutters are so easy to use and we use them so often, we tend to forget that they have the potential to cause serious injury. So although some newer models come with locks and shields, the best safety device is your own attention to what you're doing.

Use an acrylic ruler that is at least 6″ × 24″ to cut the fabrics for your quilts. If you're going to purchase a ruler, consider the new 8½″ × 24″ size, because the extra width is useful. If you're going to buy more than one ruler, try to stick with one brand if possible, since minute variations between manufacturers can result in imprecise cuts that will have to be remedied later. Check the accuracy of the ruler before you buy and, again, buy the best you can afford. I frequently use the

Omnigrid 98L triangle ruler. Although not created for these purposes, it is a good size for cutting starting triangles on directional fabric or as a template for fussy-cutting them. A shorter ruler (4″ × 14″ or 6″ × 12″) is convenient for cutting strips and segments, and Glow-line tape is useful when marking your rulers at odd increments.

You will also need basic sewing supplies such as pins, scissors, and a good-quality 50-weight cotton thread in a neutral color and medium value for piecing. A lot depends on the strength of your thread, so don't try to save money—you'll pay for it later.

Use a mechanical pencil for marking the braids, since the line is thin and the point stays sharp. If the graphite line won't show on darker fabrics, I prefer a Verithin silver or yellow marking pencil; you will also need a pencil sharpener for these because they wear down quickly.

Continuous access to an ironing board and iron is also essential.

In addition to the above necessities, there are a few more items that will be helpful. A reducing glass (the opposite of a magnifying glass) enables you to get an overall look at your project, and a previously unnoticed fabric will sometimes stand out as too bright or off in color when viewed as if from afar. A similar effect can be achieved by looking through the viewfinder of a camera, a door peephole, or the wrong end of a pair of binoculars.

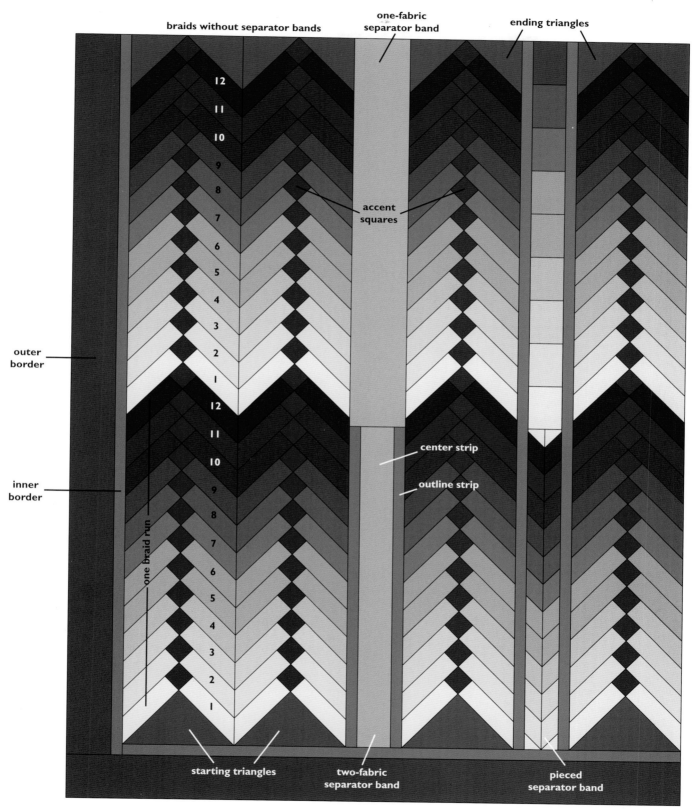

Anatomy of a French Braid

2 Fabric Selection

When selecting fabric for most quilts, quilters often build around one main fabric, adding others to accent that favorite. But in French braid quilts, you are trying to achieve a look in which the fabrics blend, so there isn't a main fabric to rely on. Instead, these quilts usually require the selection of several starter fabrics. The gaps between the starters are filled to complete the braid run. Then fabrics are selected for the accent squares, starting triangles, and, possibly, ending triangles. Fabric decisions for other parts of the quilt are made as the need arises.

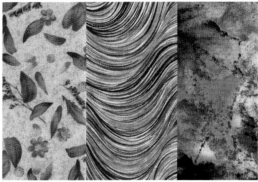

Starter fabric groups

A collection that might work well

Braid-Run Fabrics

The most challenging part of fabric selection for French braid quilts is the choice of fabrics for the braid run; and this choice is a prerequisite for all your other choices. However, because the most challenging selection comes first, the rest will seem easy!

Choose a run of ten to twelve fabrics that shade gradually from light to dark, or from color to color, or both. In the basic braid, this run occurs twice in each braid strip, but there are many possible variations. When the fabrics are laid out in order, the run should appear to change in value or color smoothly, without noticeable gaps. Each fabric should appear to pour into the next, much as areas of wet paint might blend together where they touch. And because the first fabric will abut the last where the run begins its repeat, those two fabrics must also harmonize.

Every quilter knows that finding the perfect fabric is sometimes impossible. Because your eye perceives the shading as gradual, your eyes will see it that way even if the sequence has minor jumps in color or value.

The easiest way to begin fabric selection for the braid run is to find three or four fabrics you like and that seem to blend well. These "starters" are usually in the same color family or in related color families.

A fabric collection by a single manufacturer can be quite useful, especially if the prints are of varying scales and values in harmonizing colors.

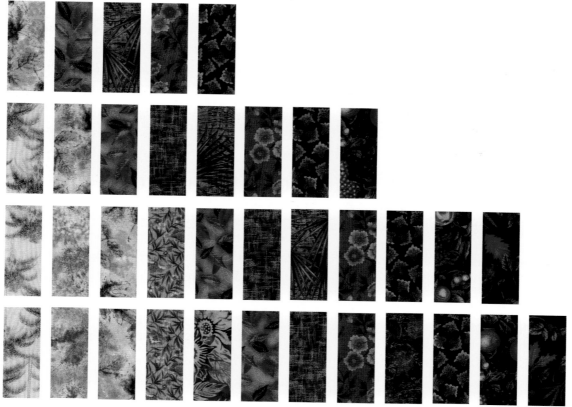

Building the braid run

Arrange your fabrics in the order in which you think they will appear in the braid, usually light to dark. Look at the arrangement critically to decide where other fabrics are needed; your goal is to arrange them so that they flow together. Add, subtract, and intersperse other fabrics until you get the effect you are seeking.

While the fabrics are still on the bolt, it is easy to overlook the fact that one in particular may be brighter or duller than the rest, so you'll have to be discriminating in your choices. Step back about six or eight feet periodically, since the effect from farther away is different from the effect when you are closer. By putting distance between yourself and the fabric, you see the prints as a group rather than as individual pieces, and you can more easily identify and replace those that don't work well.

Occasionally you may have to add a fabric that is very similar to its neighbor in order to find enough fabrics for the run.

Since you will be cutting everything into smaller pieces, be careful about using large, high-contrast prints. Stripes and plaids can work well, although they may require extra care in cutting, but avoid prints that are patterned diagonally in one direction, since the print will run horizontally on one side of the braid and vertically on the other. When selecting any directional fabric, remember that the long side of your finished braid segment will be on the lengthwise grain of the fabric, which is not what you see when you stack bolts, so be careful.

Change fabric that is too bright.

Diagonal prints will run in opposite directions.

Don't forget that the appearance of any fabric depends on its neighbors. The perfect run of seven or eight often changes dramatically with the addition of number nine. You must then decide whether to continue with the original plan or to remove some of the first eight, keep number nine, and go in a different direction. This decision usually depends on which run is easier to complete with the available choices.

Try not to become too emotionally involved with your fabric choices; it really doesn't matter if your favorite is eliminated, as long as the run works well as a whole. There will be more fabric selection in the future of this quilt, and rejected fabric can often be used at some later point. When you are satisfied, be sure to keep track of the order of the fabrics, either by naming and numbering them or by cutting swatches and taping them to a piece of paper.

Note ◆◆◆◆◆◆◆◆◆◆◆

If you are using ¼-yard pieces for a basic braid or a variation, there is no extra fabric for swatching.

There are a few other practical tips that can help you in the task of fabric selection. Don't begin when you are tired or cranky, or twenty minutes before you are due elsewhere. This is a visual process; if you have a poor sense of color, ask for help from a friend or a quilt shop employee. Try to be flexible. Finding a run of ten or twelve fabrics that flow well is not easy; if you restrict yourself in advance to a specific color scheme, you are inviting failure. Last, if you belong to the school of quilting that believes the quilter is in charge of the quilt, rather than the other way around, now is the time to reconsider your belief.

Accent Fabric

Once you have chosen the braid run, select the accent fabric. This fabric marches in little squares vertically up the center of each braid strip (see Anatomy of a French Braid, page 7). If you are trying to achieve a calm, subtle quilt, pick something with a low degree of contrast or something in the same color family as the braid fabrics. If you want a more exciting look, a stronger or brighter accent will be better.

Examine your braid run. If there is a common color in the majority of the fabrics, start there. Lay various bolts of fabric in that color next to the run. Try to find one that has only one or two colors and is not very busy, though a geometric print can sometimes work. Remember that prints will be oriented diagonally in the finished quilt. Don't worry if your accent fabric fades into one or two of your braid fabrics. Your eye will see the accents as a continuous line whether or not each square is clearly visible.

If one color doesn't work, try a different one. A slight change in the accent fabric can make a big difference in the look of the finished quilt, so don't be afraid to try unlikely colors (*Braid Runners 1–4*, page 35). Again, this is not your last chance for fabric selection; you still might use today's rejects tomorrow.

Triangle Fabrics

You have chosen fabric for your braid run and your accent squares, but you still need fabrics for the starting and ending triangles. These fabrics appear only at the bottom and top edges of your quilt, so they are not its focus; but several types of prints work better than others.

In either area, nondirectional overall prints are best. For the starting triangles, directional prints and one-way designs can also work if cut carefully, though extra fabric may be needed. Do not use obviously linear prints, plaids, or stripes. Solids may be boring in these larger areas, but a mottled look can work well. For the ending triangles, do not use any type of directional print unless you are willing to fussy cut each triangle.

Good choices for triangles

Poor choices for triangles

Note ◆◆◆◆◆◆◆◆◆◆◆◆

You can't begin sewing the braid until you've chosen the starting triangle fabric. However, since you do not use the ending triangle fabric until the rest of the braid strip is constructed, you may want to complete the braids up to that point before selecting this fabric.

Think about color and value. If your braid run shades from light to dark, the lightest fabric in the braid run will be the first fabric sewn onto the starting triangle; the darkest fabric in the braid run will be the last sewn onto the braid strip before adding the ending triangles. You have three options in selecting your triangles. First, you can make your starting triangle lighter than the lightest braid fabric and the ending triangles darker than the darkest (*Lucy's Leftover Watercolor Kit*, page 20). This option means that you are actually picking a run of fourteen. Also, your quilt will be very light at one end and very dark at the other, which can make border selection more difficult.

The second choice is to start with a dark triangle fabric, add the braid runs from light to dark and finish with light triangles (*Formal Affair*, page 22). This option results in a better value distribution, and is also easier to select. The beginning dark triangle doesn't have to be darker than the darkest fabric in the braid run, and the ending triangles don't have to be lighter than the lightest braid-run fabric. And since both ends of the braid are similar in appearance, finding borders is often easier with this method than with the previous one.

The third, and simplest, option is to use the same (usually medium-value) fabric for both the starting and ending triangles (*Passion for Purple*, page 30). A lighter or darker fabric can sometimes be used effectively as long as there is enough contrast at both ends (*Baby Braid*, page 32). Using the same fabric for both sets of triangles also makes the borders easier to pick, since there is one less fabric with which they must coordinate.

Remember, at this point you need fabric only for the starting triangles. If you think that you may want to use the same fabric for the ending triangles, buy extra. Once you've selected your fabrics, you are ready to cut and sew your braid strips. Go to Chapter 3—Basic French Braid Construction.

When your braid strips are finished, decide whether or not to add separator bands. If you decide not to add the separator bands, go to page 17.

Separator-Band Fabrics

Separator bands divide the quilt into sections and accentuate the braid strips. They also widen the quilt, but there is a limit to how wide they can be before they overwhelm the braids. To choose fabrics for the separator bands, take the braid strips with you to visit your local quilt shop. Swatches will not help you, nor will a verbal description of your color scheme. Take the braids with you.

Look at the quilts in this book and decide whether you want one fabric or two for your separators. It is usually easier to pick a two-fabric band than to find a single fabric that works well, and most people seem to prefer the former look. If you want only one fabric, you'll get the best results with a band fabric that is the same as or similar to the accent fabric (*Baby Braid*, page 32).

Selecting fabric for two-fabric separator bands is like choosing borders. The outline strip of the separator band stops the eye and highlights a color, and the center strip unites everything. Occasionally the accent fabric can be used for the outline strips of the band, but be careful because it can become too dominant if reused. Usually, there are a few possible choices, but if not, think back to the fabrics you rejected as accents and try them here. Don't worry if your chosen fabric fades into the braids at some point in the run; however, if the fabric blends in everywhere, keep looking. If you discover several possible options for the outline strip, keep them handy while you select the center strip.

The center strip of the separator band is wider than the outline strip. Nebulously patterned prints are often best, though there are exceptions (*It's Always Green in Miami,* page 40). Find several fabrics, each with a few braid strip colors that you wish to highlight. Audition each of these in combination with each outline strip candidate and with all areas of the braid strips before deciding.

If you choose to make a pieced separator band, as in Chapter 6 (pages 49–69), be sure you allow for this extra fabric when you select your braid-run fabrics.

Border Fabrics

Border selection for French braid quilts is as for any other quilt. Look for a fabric that complements the rest of your quilt without taking it over. You may be able to reuse an accent or separator band fabric for one or more borders. Select this fabric after the braids are completed and sewn into a top, with or without separator bands. Audition your prospects individually and in various combinations.

3 Basic French Braid Construction

The basic French braid quilt is constructed from four identical braid strips, each made of two runs of the braid sequence (Anatomy of a French Braid, page 7). The finished length of the braid strips is about 62″ for the ten-fabric version or about 73″ for twelve fabrics. The finished width of each braid is approximately 11″. Although the basic process is the same for all the projects in this book, individual measurements and project instructions vary. If the project you like is not the proper size, Chapter 7 will help you adjust the quilt to your own requirements.

The two basic parts of French braid quilts, the braid strips and the separator bands, are sewn as separate units before being joined together. The construction of each will be discussed individually, and each step will be explained, so you'll be able to refer back to this chapter and the next if you have a problem.

Cutting the Braid-Run Fabrics

You have selected ten to twelve fabrics for your braid run. Before cutting any of the fabric, make sure there is at least 40″ of useable width in each piece. If you are using fat quarters, you must have 20″ of useable width from the selvage to the opposite edge. If any fabric is not wide enough, buy an extra ¼ yard.

1. Arrange the fabrics in their prospective order.

2. Cut a strip 8½″ × width of fabric from every braid fabric; then cut each strip in half so that you have 2 pieces, each 8½″ × 20+″. OR, from fat quarters, cut 2 strips, from selvage to center, 8½″ wide. Be sure to cut in the right direction.

3. Keeping the fabric strips in the order of the braid run, make 2 piles by placing one 8½″ × 20+″ piece of each braid fabric into each pile.

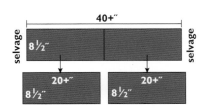

Cutting 40″-wide braid fabrics

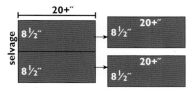

Cutting fat quarters

4. Set aside one of the piles of fabric. From each piece of fabric in the other pile, cut 2 segments 2½″ wide, stacking the braid fabrics to cut several at once, if you prefer. Set these aside for now.

Stack and cut one pile of braid segments.

Cutting the Starting Triangles

The cutting instructions for the starting triangles vary with the type and configuration of the fabric. Fat quarters can be used only with nondirectional prints. Cut a 13″ × 13″ square and then cut the square in half diagonally twice, to yield 4 quarter-square triangles.

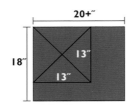

Starting triangles from fat quarter

A straight quarter must be used for directional fabrics (you want the print to run up and down but not sideways) and may be used for nondirectional fabrics. Cut one strip 6½″ × width of fabric; then use a 45-45-90° triangle ruler to cut 4 triangles, turning the ruler 180° after each cut. Do not use a fat quarter for directional fabrics unless you don't mind that the motif will be horizontal in 2 of your triangles.

Starting triangles from directional fabric or nondirectional straight yardage

Triangles from fabric with a one-way design, such as a print in which the pattern points in only one direction, must be cut from 2 strips 6½″ wide. Buy extra fabric and use your triangle ruler (page 6) to cut all the triangles in the same direction.

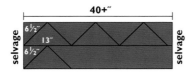

Starting triangles from one-way print

If you are fussy cutting a particular motif, cut each triangle separately. An Omnigrid 98L triangle ruler works well as a template—it's slightly larger than you need,

but you will trim the fabric later anyway. To determine the amount of fabric needed, spread it out and count the available motifs.

Laying Out the Braid

At this point, we must take an essential detour to lay out the braid pieces and examine the overall effect. If you are very good with color or anxious to begin sewing, you will be tempted to omit this step. If that's how you feel, please stop, take a Zen cleansing breath, reconsider, and at least read this section before deciding to ignore it.

Lay one of the starting triangles on a table with the longest side closest to you (or at about knee level on a design wall). Fold the accent fabric into a long strip and lay it out so it stretches from the top of the triangle upward. Now take the 2 sets of 2½″ × 8½″ braid segments that you set aside earlier and lay them out in the predetermined order, beginning at the top of the starting triangle and continuing until you have laid out one entire run. Leave space at the center between the braid segments to let the accent fabric show through.

Lay out the braid run.

Troubleshooting

Take some time to look at your results critcally—this is your chance to change things without having to rip. If necessary, rearrange the fabrics until you are satisfied with their placement. If you change the order of the run, do so on only one side of the braid so you'll be able to compare the result to your original plan. Look carefully and take your time; a reducing glass may be helpful. Usually the placement of the fabrics is fine; but if you find yourself rearranging the fabrics several times, the problem is usually due to one of three causes.

- If one fabric pops out of the progression, it is usually because it's the wrong value (too light or too dark), the wrong hue (color), or the wrong intensity (to bright or too dull) (photo, bottom of page 9). If any of these issues arise, move, replace, or eliminate the offending fabric. In the basic braid, each fabric you eliminate will decrease the total length by slightly less than 6″. (Before tossing anything, however, check the reverse side—sometimes the difference is just enough to make the fabric workable.)

- If you can't decide which of two adjacent fabrics is lighter or darker, or if two or three are so similar that they are difficult to tell apart, the order doesn't usually make much difference. You can eliminate one. If you leave them as they are, part of your braid strip may read as a large area of one color, but that's not necessarily a problem (*Cornucopia*, page 28).

- If you have a candidate for the ending triangles, lay it out also. But remember that if you're unsure of that choice, you can still change your mind after the braids are constructed.

When you have changed everything that needs changing, pick up all the pieces, return them to their original pile, and cut 6 more 2½″ segments from each fabric in that pile, for a total of 8 from each fabric.

Cutting the Accent Fabric

You must have 40″ of useable width for the accent fabric.

1. Cut strips 2½″ × width of fabric (5 strips if you are using 10 braid fabrics; 6 strips if you are using 11 or 12 braid fabrics).

2. Cut each strip in half to yield 2 pieces, each 2½″ × 20+″. If you are using 2 fat quarters, cut 2½″ strips, from the selvage to the center (20+″); cut the same number of strips as you have braid fabrics. Be sure to cut in the right direction.

3. Put all the cut accent strips with the pile of uncut braid fabrics.

Cutting the Ending Triangles

If you have selected fabric for the ending triangles, you can cut them either now or later. I usually cut later, but whenever you cut, you will need 4 squares 7″ × 7″. Cut these squares in half diagonally to yield 8 half-square triangles.

Sewing the Braids

Use a consistent ¼″ seam allowance.

Accent and Braid Fabrics

1. Sew a half-strip of accent fabric to each 8½″ × 20+″ piece of braid fabric in the uncut pile, matching the long sides. Press the seams toward the braid fabrics (the larger pieces), no matter which fabric is darker.

2. Subcut each of these accented braid fabric units into 8 segments 2½″ × 10½″ each.

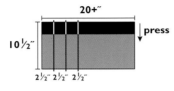

20+″

10½″

↓ press

2½″ 2½″ 2½″

Subcutting braid segments

Braid Strips

1. Lay out a starting triangle right side up, with the longest side closest to you. As you add the braid strips remember to always sew with the new piece on top as the fabric goes through the sewing machine. This is essential to ensure that both sides of your braid finish close to the same length.

2. Lay an unaccented 2½″ × 8½″ segment of the first braid fabric right side down on the left short side of the triangle, matching the 90° angles at the top of the triangle. The side of the triangle will be longer than the segment. Pin if you like, rotate the triangle, and then sew toward the 90° angle, keeping the braid segment on top.

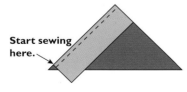

Start sewing here.

Sewing first braid segment

3. Sew a braid segment onto each of the other 3 triangles in the same way, using a chain-piecing method.

4. Press the seam toward the braid segment. Throughout the piecing of the braid strips, press the seam toward the latest piece you have added. Finger-pressing is not satisfactory; use an iron.

5. Lay an accented 2½″ × 10½″ segment of the first braid fabric face down on the right short side of the triangle, matching the seamlines and top 90° angles. If you have sewn and pressed correctly, your top (90° angle) edges will meet and your seam allowances will nest together nicely. If the top edges don't quite match when you butt the seams, match the seamlines, not the edges. The segment will again be shorter than the side of your triangle. Sew from the top of the accent square (the 90° angle) to the bottom of the segment, keeping the new piece on top.

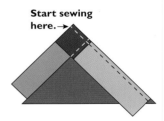

Start sewing here. →

Sewing second braid segment

6. Repeat for the other 3 triangles and press all the seams toward the new segments.

7. Add the remaining braid fabrics in the same manner, alternating the plain and accented segments of each fabric.

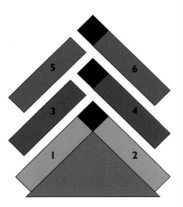

Piecing sequence

8. When you have used all the fabrics once, return to the first fabric and continue through the series again. You should not have any braid segments left.

9. Pick up one of the ending triangles and, placing the right sides together, line up its long side with the left side of the top of the braid strip. Leave about ¾″ of the triangle hanging off the edge at the top of the braid, rather than the usual ¼″. If the 90° angle of the triangle points to the braid seam that is second from the top of the braid, you're in the right spot. The braid segment is longer than the triangle edge, but don't worry; the triangle has been sized to allow for later trimming.

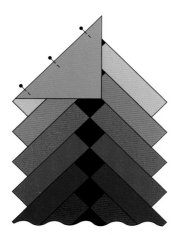

Alignment for ending triangle

10. Pin the edges together to avoid stretching the bias; flip the entire unit over so that the triangle is on the bottom, and sew. Repeat for the other 3 braid strips and press the seams toward the triangles. Repeat the process with the remaining 4 triangles on the top right side of the braid.

Congratulations! Your braid strips are finished.

Trimming Braids Without Separator Bands

To sew the braid strips together, you must convert the dog-eared edges into straight lines. You will need a table with a gridded cutting mat, a ruler that is at least 6″ × 24″, and a rotary cutter. If you have a cutting table and mat that are long enough to accommodate the entire length of a braid strip, use them. If your space is limited to the length of a shorter rotary cutting mat, work in sections.

1. Press the braid. Begin at the starting triangle and press toward the top, using a side-to-side motion. This will help eliminate any pleats in the seamlines while also preventing possible stretching caused by pressing along the length of the braid.

2. The grainline is on the diagonal (bias) now, so your braids will flex crosswise very easily. Carefully lay the braid right side up on the cutting mat, smoothing it as flat as possible without stretching it lengthwise. If you cannot spread it out full length, start at the ending triangle section and accordion fold the other end of the braid gently at the opposite end of the mat. Without letting either end of the braid hang off the edge of the table, align the outside points of one of your zigzag edges with a line on the mat.

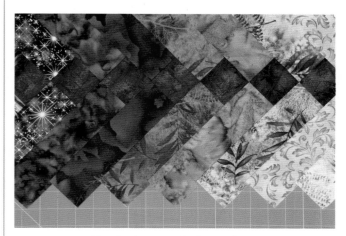

Align the dog ears with a line on the mat.

3. Determine your cutting line by measuring out from the centermost corners of the accent squares to the side of the braid. The edge of your braid is still a zigzag, so measure to the inside of the "zag"—the farthest you can go without running out of fabric. Measure each braid in several places and in both directions, because these numbers may vary. Use the smallest of these measurements, usually 5½"–5¾" (depending on your seam allowances), as the measurement to line up and trim each side of the braid.

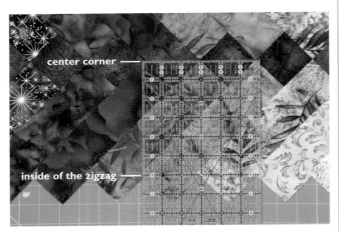

Measure from the center out.

4. Keep the outer points of one side of the braid lined up with a mat line; align a long line on your 24" ruler (usually the ¼" or ½" line on a 6"-wide ruler) with the centermost corners of the accent squares.

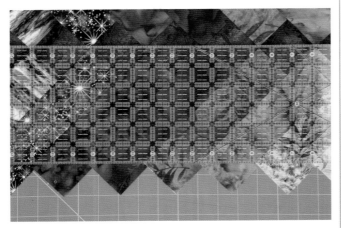

Align the ruler for cutting or marking.

If you find that a few of the center corners don't line up with your ruler, you can pull the braid gently until they do so. Do not pull on the side of the braid directly adjacent to the non-aligned corner; instead you must pull on the end of the seam that attaches the misaligned accent square to the braid run. If you are still unable to align the accent squares, you may have cut an accent rectangle instead of a square. Look carefully and measure to make sure.

Adjust misaligned accent square.

5. Once your braid is properly aligned along the 24" length of your ruler, use your rotary cutter to trim the edges. Cut only 12"–18" at a time because no matter how careful you have been, the braid will not always lie perfectly straight. Before moving the braid strip, place the ruler on the opposite edge, realign it with the center squares at the same distance on the ruler as in Step 4, and trim.

Trim the braid.

6. Before moving this top section of the braid, trim the ending triangles. Use a ruler at least 6″ wide and align one set of crosswise ruler lines with each of the edges you just cut. The ¼″ ruler line at the top of the braid strip must meet the top point of the top accent square. Recheck to make sure that your ¼″ line is at the top point, and then use your rotary cutter to trim across the top of the braid.

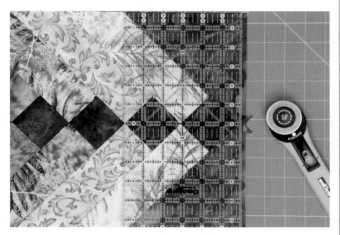

Trim ending triangles.

7. Work your way down the braid strip, measuring and trimming as many times as necessary. If you are unable to lay out the entire strip at once, roll up the trimmed end and unfold the untrimmed portion as you go. Remember that once you have trimmed the edges, they are on the bias, so do not let the end of the braid strip dangle from the edge of the table.

8. When you finish trimming the sides of the braid strip, trim the starting triangles. Trim from the point where your cut side intersects your very first braid segment seam, across to the corresponding point on the opposite side of the braid. This line will not always be parallel to the bottom edge of your starting triangle.

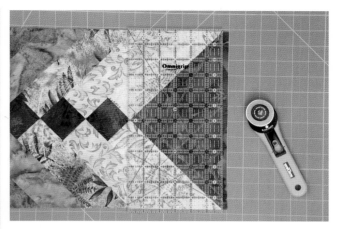

Trim starting triangles.

9. After you trim an entire strip, carry it gently to the sewing machine and staystitch the bias sides within the seam allowances—about ⅛″ from each edge. Trim the other 3 strips similarly, staystitching each braid after you cut it.

Sewing Braids Together

You are now ready to sew the braid strips together. Since all the seam allowances are facing the same direction, you cannot butt the seams. Pin every seam intersection, using more than one pin if necessary.

1. Stitch the seam, preferably not at top speed. Check the seam intersections on the right side; if you are satisfied, press this seam open.

2. Sew pairs of the braids together. Press the seams open, and then sew these larger units together and press again. Once you have sewn the 4 braids together, finish your top by adding borders, referring to page 73 if necessary.

1 Lucy's Leftover Watercolor Kit

Basic Braid without Separators

FINISHED SIZE: 55″ × 74″

Fabric Requirements

Purchase now

- ½ yard each of 10 fabrics for braid run —fat quarters okay

- ½ yard for accent squares—2 fat quarters okay

- ¼ yard for starting triangles—fat quarter okay if nondirectional (½ yard for one-way directional fabric)

- ¼ yard nondirectional for ending triangles—fat quarter okay (½ yard for one-way directional fabric)

Purchase later

- ⅜ yard for inner borders

- 1 yard for outer borders (1⅞ yards if you prefer not to piece)

- 3½ yards for backing if pieced crosswise (4½ yards if pieced lengthwise)

- ½ yard for binding

- 59″ × 78″ batting

Note ◆◆◆◆◆◆◆◆◆◆◆◆

Basic French braid quilts can be made using only ¼ yard of each braid fabric rather than the ½ yard listed. Since this assumes that every fabric has at least 40″ of useable width and that you make NO errors in cutting, I recommend that you purchase ½ yard. But if there is only ¼ yard (fat or not) of one of your fabrics, buy it and cut carefully.

Cutting

Refer to pages 13–15 for basic instructions.

BRAIDS: From each fabric, cut one strip 8½″ × width of fabric; then cut the strips in half. OR, from each fat quarter, cut 2 strips, from selvage to center, 8½″ wide.

ACCENTS: Cut 5 strips 2½″ × width of fabric; then cut the strips in half. OR, from fat quarters, cut 10 strips, from selvage to center, 2½″ wide.

STARTING TRIANGLES: Cut 4 quarter-square triangles, each with a 13″ base.

ENDING TRIANGLES: Cut 4 squares 7″ × 7″; then cut the squares in half diagonally to obtain 8 half-square triangles.

INNER BORDERS: Cut 6 strips 1½″ × width of fabric.

OUTER BORDERS: Cut 7 strips 5″ × length of fabric. OR, cut 4 strips 5″ × length of fabric if you purchased enough for unpieced borders.

Construction

Refer to pages 13–19 for basic instructions.

1. Separate the braid fabrics into 2 piles (page 13).

2. From one pile, cut 2 segments 2½″ wide from each fabric. Audition the segments with the accent and triangle fabrics; rearrange or replace as needed (pages 14–15). Cut 6 more segments from each fabric in the first pile.

3. Sew an accent strip to each fabric in the second pile of braid fabrics (page 16). Subcut the fabric pairs into 8 segments 2½″ wide.

4. Construct the braids (pages 16–17).

5. Trim and staystitch the braids (pages 17–19).

6. Sew the braids together (page 19).

7. Construct and attach the borders (page 73).

8. Construct the backing; layer the top with the batting and backing (page 73). Quilting suggestions are on page 72.

9. Make the binding and bind (page 74).

2 Formal Affair

FINISHED SIZE: 52½″ × 82″

Quilted by Barbara Lacey

Formal Affair differs from the usual French braid only in that the accent fabrics and the braid segments both change. Choose the black-and-white braid-run fabric first, then the color-wheel accent fabrics. Decide the order of the accents and assign each to its respective braid fabric. You need one half-strip of each accent fabric (2½″ × 20+″), so scraps can be used. The backs of black-on-color or tone-on-tone prints will often work well to create the gradations in the accents.

Fabric Requirements

Purchase now

- ½ yard each of 12 black-and-white fabrics for braid run—fat quarters okay

- Scraps of 12 fabrics for accent squares, each at least 2½″ × 20+″

- ¼ yard for starting triangles—fat quarter okay if nondirectional (½ yard for one-way directional)

- ¼ yard nondirectional fabric for ending triangles—fat quarter okay (½ yard for one-way directional)

Purchase later

- Scraps of 2 or more accent or similar fabrics to total 16 pieces at least 2″ × 2″ for border cornerstones

- ⅛ yard or leftover strip at least 3½″ wide of one black-and-white fabric for border cornerstones

- 1⅛ yards for outer borders (2⅛ yards if you prefer not to piece)

- 5 yards for backing (pieced lengthwise)

- ⅝ yard for binding

- 57″ × 86″ batting

Note ◆◆◆◆◆◆◆◆◆◆◆

Basic French Braid quilts may be made using only ¼ yard of each braid fabric rather than the ½ yard listed. Since this assumes that every fabric has at least 40″ of useable width and that you will make NO errors in cutting, I recommend that you purchase ½ yard. But if there is only ¼ yard (fat or not) of one of your fabrics, buy it and cut carefully.

Cutting

Refer to pages 13–15 for basic instructions.

BRAIDS: From each fabric, cut one strip 8½″ × width of fabric; then cut the strips in half. OR, from each fat quarter, cut 2 strips, from selvage to center, 8½″ wide.

ACCENTS: From each fabric, cut one strip 2½″ × 20+″.

STARTING TRIANGLES: Cut 4 quarter-square triangles, each with a 13″ base.

ENDING TRIANGLES: Cut 4 squares 7″ × 7″; then cut the squares in half diagonally to obtain 8 half-square triangles.

BORDER CORNERSTONES: From each of 2 accent fabrics, cut a strip 2″ × 17+″. OR, cut 16 squares 2″ × 2″ from various scraps.

BORDER CORNERSTONES, BLACK-AND-WHITE: Cut one strip 3½″; subcut the strip into 8 squares 3½″ × 3½″. Cut the squares in half diagonally to yield 16 half-square triangles.

BORDERS: Cut 7 strips 4¾″ × length of fabric. OR, cut 4 strips 4¾″ × length of fabric if you purchased enough for unpieced borders.

Construction

Refer to pages 13–19 for basic instructions.

1. Separate the braid fabrics into 2 piles (page13).

2. From one pile, cut 2 segments 2½″ wide from each fabric. Audition the segments with the accent and triangle fabrics; rearrange or replace as needed (pages 14–15). Cut 6 more segments from each fabric in the first pile.

3. Sew each fabric in the second pile of braid fabrics to its pre-assigned accent strip (page 16). Subcut the fabric pairs into 8 segments 2½″ wide.

4. Construct the braids (pages 16–17).

5. Trim and staystitch the braids (pages 17–19).

6. Sew the braids together (page 19).

7. For the border cornerstones, sew the 2 strips 2″ wide of scrap accent fabrics together, matching the long edges and pressing the seam toward the darker fabric. Cut the fabric pair into 8 segments 2″ wide; sew the segments into 4 four-patches. OR, sew pairs of precut 2″ squares together; sew these units into 4 four-patches.

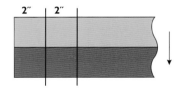

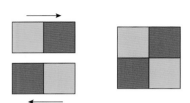

8. Sew one pair of black-and-white triangles onto 2 opposite sides of each four-patch. Sew the black-and-white triangles onto the remaining 2 sides of the four-patches. Press all the seams toward the triangles. Trim to 4¾″ × 4¾″, centering the four-patch.

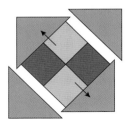

9. Construct the borders by measuring the length and width of the quilt and then cutting the borders to those lengths (page 73). Sew a cornerstone from Step 8 onto each end of each top and bottom border.

10. Attach the borders (page 73).

11. Construct the backing; layer the top with the batting and backing (page 73). Quilting suggestions are on page 72.

12. Make the binding and bind (page 74).

4 Adding Basic Separator Bands

Marking the Braids

You may choose to add separator bands to your French braid quilt; they will change both the size and the look of the quilt. Before you can construct the separator bands, you must determine their eventual length. To do that, you must first mark and measure the braid strips. Refer to Trimming Braids Without Separator Bands (Steps 1–4, pages 17–18) except, you will mark a line on your braid strips to add separator bands. Do not trim the zigzag edges off as you would if you were not adding separator bands.

1. Press the braids, measure them, and align the ruler (pages 17–18). Draw a pencil line (do not trim). Since the fabric shifts easily, make short overlapping pencil strokes. As you move the pencil down the length of the braid, move your other hand along with the pencil so that the hand on the ruler is always adjacent to your pencil, and the fabric is stationary where you are marking.

Line marked on braid strip

Note ◆◆◆◆◆◆◆◆◆◆◆◆◆

Theoretically, your marked line will always align perfectly with the end of your ruler when you move it to the next section of braid. But no matter how carefully you align and mark the braid, parts of it seem to resist straightening. Occasionally you will move and realign your ruler only to find that the end of the ruler does not meet the line you have just drawn. If this happens, first check to make sure that none of your segments has been miscut. If they are all correct, back up your ruler a few inches so that, rather than meeting the very end of your pencil mark, it overlaps the pencil line by a few inches. Realign the ruler with the center squares; the end of the ruler should now meet part of the pencil line. Start your new line there and disregard the last few inches of the previous line.

2. Trim the ending and starting triangles as you mark. For the ending triangles, rather than aligning the crosswise ruler lines with the cut sides of the braid, align the ruler lines with the pencil lines you drew. Trim the starting triangles using the pencil lines, rather than the cut edges, as your reference points (Steps 6–9, page 19).

3. Measure the length of each braid from bottom to top down the center. Fold the braid in half if necessary. Write down the measurements for all 4 braids. Be careful not to stretch the braids since these measurements determine the length of your separator bands. It is not uncommon for the numbers to vary—a difference of up to ¾″ will still work in fairly easily.

Cutting the Separator Bands

Separator bands should be cut on the lengthwise grain of the fabric if at all possible. However, they can be cut crosswise to take advantage of a design element, such as a stripe (*Shadow City*, page 54), or to save fabric.

Single-Fabric Separator Bands

1. Decide on the width of a single-fabric separator band by laying your braids on a piece of the candidate fabric. Move the braids around and look at the effect of various widths of separator bands, making sure that the bands don't overshadow the braids.

2. When you have determined the finished width, add ½″ to this width for seam allowances, and then cut the number of strips you need. Seam strips if necessary to obtain a strip slightly longer than the longest braid. Press the seams in either direction. Proceed to Getting It All Together.

Two-Fabric Separator Bands

1. For two-fabric separator bands, I most often use finished widths of 1″ for the outline strips and 2″ for the center strip of each separator band. Cut 2 strips 1½″ wide of the outline fabric and one strip 2½″ wide of the center fabric, each slightly longer than the longest braid. If your fabric is not long enough to cut these strips in one piece, seam shorter strips together as needed. Press these seams in either direction.

2. To make each separator band, sew a long outline strip to each side of a center strip, all slightly longer than your longest braid. Press the seams either toward the center strip or toward the outline strips.

Getting It All Together

1. The lengths of the braid strips are rarely the same, so you will have to pick a measurement that is neither the largest nor the smallest—you must be able to ease both the longest and shortest braids into this length.

2. Cut all the separator bands to the length you have selected. Recheck your notes and the separator band lengths to make sure they are all the same.

3. Find the centers of the separator bands by folding them in half; mark the center in the seam allowances on both long edges of each band. Find the quarters in the same way by folding the ends to meet the centers; mark and set the bands aside.

4. Next, find the approximate lengthwise centers of the braid strips by folding each braid strip in half, matching the ends at their center points. Place a pin at the center fold on each side of each braid.

5. Open out each braid strip and examine the pin placement. Your center pins will not fall at exactly the same spot on all the braids. In fact, even pins on opposite sides of the same braid strip may fall in different places. If that is the case, select a spot in the braid run that is close to the center fold of each braid strip. For example, you might decide that a place on your marked line that is ½″ above a particular seam would make a good universal center. Whatever method you use to determine the center, it is important that you use the same center on each braid, so that the segments line up across the width of the finished quilt. Use a pencil to mark the center on both sides of each braid strip outside your marked line.

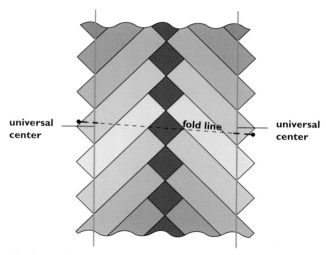

Pins do not fall at the same center point on both sides of the braid. Select a common point and mark this as your universal center.

6. Find the quarters by folding the ends of the each braid to your chosen center. Adjust all your quarter marks so that they occur at the same place in the braid run on each braid strip, just as you did for the centers.

7. Keeping the separator on top, pin the center of the separator band to the center mark on one of the braid strips. Match the long raw edge of the separator band to the pencil line on the braid strip, pinning the ends of the separator band to the ends of the braid strip and at the quarter marks. Lay out the whole unit on a table and gently adjust the braid strip so that it fits to the separator. If your braid doesn't want to fit, or if you have to stretch it to make it fit, measure again to make sure that you have cut your separator bands to the correct length and that you have marked the halves and quarters correctly on the braid strip. Pin at every braid seam.

Pin the separator band to the braid strip.

8. Attach a ¼"-seam presser foot to your sewing machine. Use the raw edge of the separator band as your guide to sew the band to the braid strip, keeping the separator on top. Sew at a slow to moderate speed for best results.

9. After sewing the seam, take the unpressed unit back to your cutting mat. Using the raw edge of the separator band as a guide, trim the dog ears off the side of the braid strip with your ruler and rotary cutter. Press the seam toward the separator band.

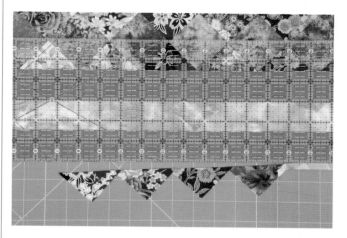

Use the edge of the separator band to trim the dog ears.

10. Repeat this entire process twice more, so that you have 3 braid strips, each with a separator band attached to the same (right or left) side.

11. Sew these bands to each other and to the unattached braid strip using the same methods for matching and pinning. Press the seams toward the separator bands.

12. Purchase everything you need to complete your quilt: fabrics for borders, backing, and binding; quilting thread; and batting. Attach the lengthwise inner borders to the 2 dog-eared outer edges of the braids in the same way, using the same lengthwise measurement as you did for the separator bands. Then add the remaining borders and finish the quilt, referring to pages 72–74 as necessary.

3 Cornucopia

Basic French Braid with Two-Fabric Separator Bands

FINISHED SIZE: 67″ × 73″

Quilted by Barbara Lacey

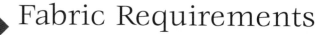

Fabric Requirements

Purchase now

- ½ yard each of 10 fabrics for braid run—fat quarters okay
- ½ yard for accent squares—fat quarters okay
- ¼ yard for starting triangles—fat quarter okay if nondirectional (½ yard for one-way directional)
- ¼ yard nondirectional fabric for ending triangles—fat quarter okay

Purchase later

- 1 yard for separator bands, center strips
- 1 yard for separator bands, outline strips
- ⅜ yard for inner borders
- 1 yard for outer borders (2 yards if you prefer not to piece)
- 4 yards for backing if pieced crosswise (4⅜ yards if pieced lengthwise)
- ⅝ yard for binding
- 71″ × 77″ batting

Note ◆◆◆◆◆◆◆◆◆◆◆

You may use only ¼ yard of each braid fabric rather than the ½ yard listed, but you must have at least 40″ of useable width and make NO errors in cutting.

Cutting

Refer to pages 13–15 for basic instructions.

BRAIDS: From each fabric, cut one strip 8½″ × width of fabric; then cut the strips in half. OR, from each fat quarter, cut 2 strips, from selvage to center, 8½″ wide.

ACCENTS: Cut 5 strips 2½″ × width of fabric; then cut the strips in half. OR, from fat quarters, cut 10 strips, from selvage to center, 2½″ wide.

STARTING TRIANGLES: Cut 4 quarter-square triangles, each with a 13″ base.

ENDING TRIANGLES: Cut 4 squares 7″ × 7″; then cut the squares in half diagonally to obtain 8 half-square triangles.

SEPARATOR BANDS, CENTER STRIPS (PAGE 26): Cut 6 strips 2½″ × length of fabric.

SEPARATOR BANDS, OUTLINE STRIPS (PAGE 26): Cut 12 strips 1½″ × length of fabric.

INNER BORDERS: Cut 6 strips 1½″ × width of fabric.

OUTER BORDERS: Cut 8 strips 5″ × length of fabric. OR, cut 4 strips 5″ × length of fabric if you purchased enough for unpieced borders.

Construction

Refer to pages 13–19 for basic instructions.

1. Separate the braid fabrics into 2 piles (page 13).

2. From one pile, cut 2 segments 2½″ wide from each fabric. Audition the segments with the accent and triangle fabrics; rearrange or replace as needed (pages 14–15). Cut 6 more segments from each fabric in the first pile.

3. Sew an accent strip to each fabric in the second pile of braid fabrics (page 16). Subcut the fabric pairs into 8 segments 2½″ wide.

4. Construct the braids (pages 16–17).

5. Mark the sides, trim the ends, and measure the braid lengths (page 25).

6. Construct 3 separator bands (pages 26–27).

7. Sew the separator bands to 3 braid strips.

8. Sew the braid/separator units together.

9. Construct and attach the borders (page 73).

10. Construct the backing; layer the top with the batting and backing (page 73). Quilting suggestions are on page 72.

11. Make the binding and bind (page 74).

4

Passion for Purple

Invert Color Sequence

Passion for Purple is not a basic French braid. The construction process is the same, but the total numbers, sizes, and dimensions differ.

FINISHED SIZE: 98″ × 109″

Quilted by Barbara Lacey

Fabric Requirements

Purchase now

- ⅝ yard each of fabrics #1–#11 for braid run
- 1 yard for accent squares
- ⅞ yard nondirectional fabric for starting and ending triangles

Purchase later

- 1⅜ yards for separator bands, center strips
- 1⅜ yards for separator bands, outline strips

- ¾ yard for inner borders
- 2¾ yards for outer borders
- 8½ yards for backing if pieced crosswise (9½ yards if pieced lengthwise)
- ¾ yard for binding
- 102″ × 113″ batting

Cutting

Refer to pages 13–15 for basic instructions.

BRAIDS: From each of fabrics #1–#11, cut 2 strips 9½″ × width of fabric.

ACCENTS: Cut 11 strips 2½″ × width of fabric.

STARTING/ENDING TRIANGLES: Cut 2 strips 7½″ wide and one strip 8″ wide. From the 7½″ strips, cut 5 starting triangles, each with a 15″ base, using a triangle ruler (page 14). From the 8″ strip, cut 5 squares 8″ × 8″; then cut the squares in half diagonally to obtain 10 half-square triangles.

SEPARATOR BANDS, CENTER STRIPS (PAGE 26): Cut 8 strips 3″ × length of fabric.

SEPARATOR BANDS, OUTLINE STRIPS (PAGE 26): Cut 16 strips 1¾″ × length of fabric.

INNER BORDERS: Cut 10 strips 2″ × width of fabric.

OUTER BORDERS: Cut 4 strips 6½″ × length of fabric.

Construction

Refer to pages 13–19 for basic instructions.

1. Separate the braid fabrics into 2 piles (page 13).

2. From one pile, cut 2 segments 2½″ wide from each fabric. Audition the segments with the accent and triangle fabrics; rearrange or replace as needed (pages 14–15). From the same pile, cut 13 more segments from fabrics #2–#10, and 8 more segments from fabrics #1 and #11.

3. Sew one accent strip to each fabric in the second pile of braid fabrics (page 16). Subcut fabrics #2–#10 into 15 segments 2½″ wide, and subcut fabrics #1 and #11 into 10 segments 2½″ wide.

4. Construct the braids (pages 16–17). For 3 braids, start with fabric #1 and continue through fabric #11; followed by fabrics #10 through #1, then by #2 through #11. For 2 braids, reverse the sequence: fabrics #11 through #1, #2 through #11, and #10 through #1. Do not repeat fabric #1 or #11 when you reverse the order in the run.

5. Mark the sides, trim the ends, and measure the braid lengths (page 25). The measurement from the center to the edge of the braid strip will be 6″–6½″.

6. Construct 4 separator bands (pages 26–27).

7. Sew the separator bands to 4 braid strips.

8. Sew the braid/separator units together.

9. Construct and attach the borders (page 73).

10. Construct the backing; layer the top with the batting and backing (page 73). Quilting suggestions are on page 72.

11. Make the binding and bind (page 74).

5

Baby Braid

Baby Braid is not a basic French braid. The construction process is the same, but the total numbers, sizes, and dimensions differ.

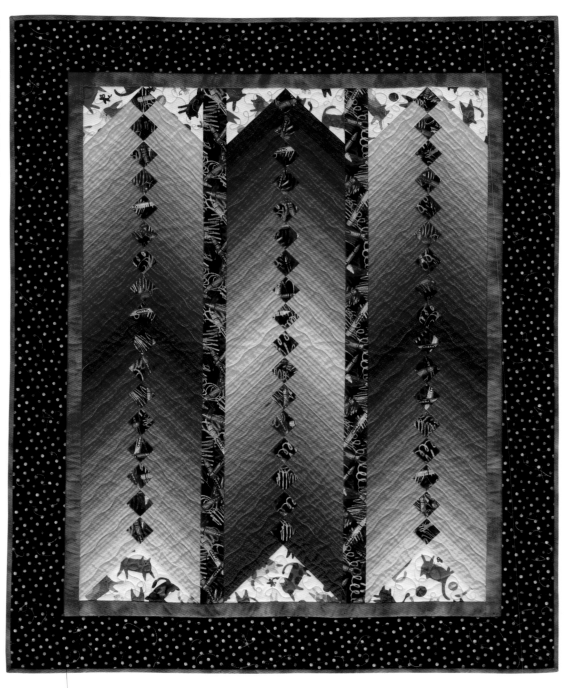

FINISHED SIZE: 37″ × 44″

Quilted by Barbara Lacey

Fabric Requirements

Purchase now

♦ ¼ yard each of 9 fabrics for braid run—fat quarters okay

♦ ¼ yard for accent squares

♦ ¼ yard nondirectional fabric for starting and ending triangles—fat quarter okay

Purchase later

♦ ¼ yard for separator bands (cut crosswise)

♦ ¼ yard for inner borders

♦ 1⅛ yards for outer borders

♦ 1½ yards for backing

♦ ⅜ yard for binding

♦ 41″ × 48″ batting

Cutting

BRAIDS: From each fabric, cut one strip 6½″ × width of fabric; then cut two 13″ pieces from each strip. OR, from fat quarters, cut 2 crosswise strips each 6½″; then cut the 20+″ width down to 13″.

ACCENTS: Cut 3 strips 1¾″ × width of fabric; then subcut each strip into 3 pieces, each at least 1¾″ × 13″.

STARTING/ENDING TRIANGLES: From ¼ yard, cut one strip 5½″ wide. Cut 3 squares 5½″ × 5½″; then cut the squares in half diagonally to yield 6 half-square triangles. Cut the rest of the strip down to 5¼″; then cut 3 starting triangles, each with a 10½″ base, using a triangle ruler (page 14). OR, from a fat quarter, cut one strip 5½″ wide; then cut one square 10½″ × 10½″ from the remaining fabric. From the 5½″ strip, cut 3 squares 5½″; then cut the squares in half diagonally to yield 6 half-square triangles. Cut the 10½″ square in half diagonally twice to yield 4 quarter-square starting triangles; use 3 of these.

SEPARATOR BANDS (PAGE 26): Cut 2 strips 2″ × width of fabric. (The inherent stretching that occurs when separator bands are cut crosswise has less impact on smaller quilts, so the bands are cut crosswise for this quilt.)

INNER BORDERS: Cut 4 strips 1½″ × width of fabric.

OUTER BORDERS: Cut 4 strips 4″ × length of fabric.

Construction

Refer to pages 13–19 for basic instructions.

1. Separate the braid fabrics into 2 piles (page 13).

2. From one pile, cut 2 segments 1¾″ wide from each fabric. Audition with accent and triangle fabrics; rearrange or replace as needed. From the same pile, cut 4 more segments from each of fabrics #2–#8, 3 more segments from fabric #1, and 2 more from fabric #9.

3. Sew an accent strip to each fabric in the second pile of braid strip fabrics (page 16). Subcut into 1¾″ segments as follows: cut 6 segments each from fabric #2–#8; 5 from fabric #1; and 4 from fabric #9.

4. Construct the braids (pages 16–17). For 2 braids, start with fabric #1 and continue through fabric #9; then use fabrics #8 through #1. For the third braid, reverse the sequence: fabrics #9 through #1 followed by fabrics #2 through #9.

5. Mark the sides, trim the ends, and measure the braid lengths (page 25). The measurement from the center to the edge of the braid strip will be 3¾″–4¼″.

6. Cut the separator bands to the correct length (pages 26–27).

7. Sew the separator bands to 2 braid strips.

8. Sew the braid/separator units together.

9. Attach the borders (page 73).

10. Layer the top with the batting and backing (page 73). Quilting suggestions are on page 72.

11. Make the binding and bind (page 74).

5 Braid Variations

Until now you have constructed braids by starting at one end and adding segments until you arrived at the other end. There are two other ways to build the French braid strips: from the center out (*Oriental Palms*, pages 36–37) or from both ends in (*It's Always Green in Miami*, pages 40–41). In these versions, both ends of the braids look the same, so quilters who dislike the asymmetry of the basic braid might prefer these variations. And because you can do more sewing between bouts of pressing, the variations are usually quicker to construct than the basic braid. Both of the variations will add about 6″ to the length of the basic braid, for a total of approximately 79″ for the twelve-fabric version.

Center-Out French Braids

Fabric Selection

Most of the fabric selection for center-out French braids is identical to that for the basic braid. Pick the braid-run fabrics and the accent fabric first. Instead of selecting fabric for beginning triangles, choose one for center squares. This fabric will appear at the midpoint of every braid, and thus across the middle of your finished quilt, so find something that is interesting in large pieces. Don't forget that the center squares will be on the diagonal in the finished quilt, so directional fabrics may require cutting on the bias. Always cut center squares with dimensions ⅛″ less than the first cut for the braid-run fabrics. Doing so will simplify measuring and marking the width of the braids when you are ready to add the separator bands.

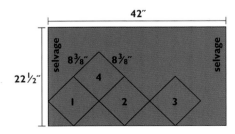

Cutting center squares from directional fabric

Select fabric for the ending triangles now or after the braid construction. Separator fabric will be selected later, as for the basic braids.

Cutting

1. Cut the braid-run and accent fabrics as for the basic braid (pages 13–15).

2. Cut 4 center squares 8⅜″ × 8⅜″.

3. Cut 8 squares 7″ × 7″ for the ending triangles; then cut the squares in half diagonally to obtain 16 half-square triangles.

Construction

The construction of center-out braids is similar to that of basic braids.

1. Start with a center square and add unaccented segments of the first fabric to the opposite sides, building from the center out in both directions. Although there are no starting triangles, the sewing sequence is the same as before.

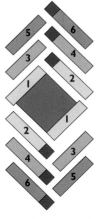

Sewing sequence for center-out braid strips

2. When the braid runs are complete, add ending triangles to both ends of each braid (steps 9–10, page 17).

3. Mark or trim the sides of the braids only after you check the braid width across the starting square. The marked (or cut) line must be ¼″ outside the outer corners of the starting square to allow for seam allowances.

4. Trim all 8 ending triangles as for the basic braid (steps 6–7, page 19).

5. Finish with or without separators. If you used a directional print for the squares, be sure that the center squares are all oriented in the same direction.

You could also make the braids into table runners at this point by adding batting and backing, quilting, and binding. Shorten your runners by using fewer fabrics. An 8-fabric runner would be about 56″ long.

Braid Runners 1–4

6 Oriental Palms

Basic Center-Out French Braid

FINISHED SIZE: 70″ × 93″

Made by Lois Willoughby, quilted by Harriet Rudoff

Fabric Requirements

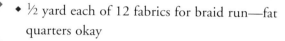

Purchase now

- ½ yard each of 12 fabrics for braid run—fat quarters okay
- ½ yard for accent squares—fat quarters okay
- ¼ yard for center squares (⅝ yard if directional)
- ½ yard nondirectional fabric for ending triangles—fat quarters okay

Purchase later

- 1¼ yards for separator bands, center strips
- 1¼ yards for separator bands, outline strips
- ½ yard for inner borders
- 2⅜ yards for outer borders
- 5½ yards for backing (pieced lengthwise)
- ¾ yard for binding
- 74″ × 97″ batting

Note ◆◆◆◆◆◆◆◆◆◆◆

You may use only ¼ yard of each braid fabric rather than the ½ yard listed, but you must have at least 40″ of useable width and make NO errors in cutting.

Cutting

Refer to Chapters 3 and 4, and pages 34–35 for basic instructions.

BRAIDS: From each fabric, cut one strip 8½″ × width of fabric; then cut the strips in half. OR, from each fat quarter, cut 2 strips, from selvage to center, 8½″ wide.

ACCENTS: Cut 6 strips 2½″ × width of fabric; then cut the strips in half. OR, from fat quarters, cut 12 strips, from selvage to center, 2½″ wide.

CENTER SQUARES: Cut 4 squares 8⅜″ × 8⅜″.

ENDING TRIANGLES: Cut 8 squares 7″ × 7″; then cut the squares in half diagonally to obtain 16 half-square triangles.

SEPARATOR BANDS, CENTER STRIPS (PAGE 26): Cut 6 strips 2½″ × length of fabric.

SEPARATOR BANDS, OUTLINE STRIPS (PAGE 26): Cut 12 strips 1½″ × length of fabric.

INNER BORDERS: Cut 8 strips 1½″ × width of fabric.

OUTER BORDERS: Cut 4 strips 6½″ × length of fabric.

Construction

Refer to Chapters 3 and 4, and pages 34–35 for basic instructions.

1. Separate the braid fabrics into 2 piles (page 13).

2. From one pile, cut 2 segments 2½″ wide from each fabric. Audition the segments with the accent and center-square fabrics; rearrange or replace as needed (pages 14–15). Cut 6 more segments from each fabric in the first pile.

3. Sew an accent strip to each fabric in the second pile of braid fabrics (page 16). Subcut the fabric pairs into 8 segments 2½″ wide.

4. Construct the braids (pages 34–35).

5. Mark the sides, trim the ends, and measure the braid lengths (page 25).

6. Sew the outline and center strips together into 3 separator bands (pages 26–27).

7. Sew the separator bands to 3 braid strips.

8. Sew the braid/separator band units together.

9. Construct and attach the border (page 73).

10. Construct the backing; layer the top with the batting and backing (page 73). Quilting suggestions are on page 72.

11. Make the binding and bind (page 74).

End-In French Braids

Fabric Selection and Cutting

For end-in French braids, the fabric selection process for the braid run, accent squares, and starting triangles is the same as for the basic braid. Picking the fabric for the ending triangles, which have now become center setting triangles, is a bit trickier. Choosing this fabric after you have sewn your braid strips is still the easiest method; however, since the fabric appears prominently across the center of the quilt, this method is a bit like working without a net. If you try it, decide in advance that later you will find just the right fabric, and look for a nondirectional one. Separator band selection is the same as for any French braid quilt.

1. Cut the braid-run and accent fabrics as you did for the basic braid (pages 13 and 15).

2. Because you need a starting triangle for each end of each braid, cut 8 triangles, not 4 (see illustrations, page 14).

3. You will need 8 center setting triangles, which are the same size as the starting triangles. The factors of directionality that you considered when cutting the starting triangles apply here (page 14), but these triangles appear vertically rather than horizontally. If necessary, cut 4 strips 6½″ lengthwise (parallel to the selvage). Use an Omnigrid 98L triangle ruler to cut 8 triangles, turning the ruler 180° after each cut. (You will need extra yardage if you cut the triangles this way.)

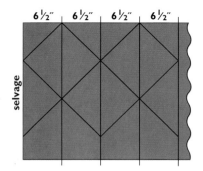

Cutting directional center setting triangles

Construction

1. Begin the end-in braid strips exactly as you would the basic braids (page 16), but sew an unaccented segment to each of 8 starting triangles, not 4. When you finish one run of the braid sequence for all 8 strips, stop.

2. To attach the center triangles, lay a braid strip face up on the table. Place a setting triangle right side down on top of it, matching the 90° angles at the top of the braid strip. The side of the triangle is shorter than the braid segment. Pin the strip to one short side of the triangle.

Aligning center setting triangle

3. Flip the unit over and sew it with the triangle on the bottom. Press the seam toward the triangle. In a similar manner, sew a triangle to the same side (left or right) of every braid strip.

Braid strips ready to be sewn together.

4. Sew pairs of braid strips together at the center triangles, placing right sides together and matching center seams. Because this seam is on the diagonal, your braid strips will be at right angles while you are sewing. Press the center seam in either direction.

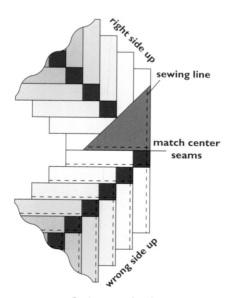

Sewing center braid seam

It's Always Green in Miami

End-In French Braid

FINISHED SIZE: 67″ × 90″

Quilted by Barbara Lacey

Fabric Requirements

Purchase now

- ½ yard each of 12 fabrics for braid run—fat quarters okay
- ½ yard for accent squares—fat quarters okay
- ½ yard for starting triangles—fat quarters okay if nondirectional
- ½ yard for center setting triangles (⅝ yard if vertically directional)

Purchase later

- 1¼ yards for separator bands, center strips
- 1¼ yards for separator bands, outline strips
- ⅜ yard for inner borders
- 1¼ yards for outer borders, cut lengthwise (2⅜ yards if you prefer not to piece)
- 5½ yards for backing (pieced lengthwise)
- ¾ yard for binding
- 71″ × 94″ batting

Note

You may use only ¼ yard of each braid fabric rather than the ½ yard listed, but you must have at least 40″ of useable width and make NO errors in cutting.

Cutting

Refer to Chapters 3 and 4, and pages 38–39 for basic instructions.

BRAIDS: From each fabric, cut one strip 8½″ × width of fabric; then cut the strips in half. OR, from each fat quarter, cut 2 strips, from selvage to center, 8½″ wide.

ACCENTS: Cut 6 strips 2½″ × width of fabric; then cut the strips in half. OR, from fat quarters, cut 12 strips, from selvage to center, 2½″ wide.

STARTING TRIANGLES: Cut 8 quarter-square triangles, each with a 13″ base.

CENTER SETTING TRIANGLES (PAGE 38): Cut 8 quarter-square triangles, each with a 13″ base.

SEPARATOR BANDS, CENTER STRIPS (PAGE 26): Cut 6 strips 2½″ × length of fabric.

SEPARATOR BANDS, OUTLINE STRIPS (PAGE 26): Cut 12 strips 1½″ × length of fabric.

INNER BORDERS: Cut 7 strips 1½″ × width of fabric.

OUTER BORDERS: Cut 8 strips 5″ × length of fabric. OR, cut 4 strips 5″ × length of fabric if you purchased enough for unpieced borders.

Construction

Refer to Chapters 3 and 4, and pages 38–39 for basic instructions.

1. Separate the braid fabrics into 2 piles (page 13).

2. From one pile, cut 2 segments 2½″ wide from each fabric. Audition the segments with the accent and beginning triangle fabrics, and the center-triangle fabric if you have it; rearrange or replace as needed (pages 14–15). Cut 6 more segments from each fabric in the first pile.

3. Sew an accent strip to each fabric in the second pile of braid strip fabrics (page 16). Subcut the fabric pairs into 8 segments 2½″ wide.

4. Construct 8 half-braids (pages 16 and 38).

5. Add the center triangles (pages 38–39).

6. Mark the sides, trim the ends, and measure the braid lengths (page 25).

7. Construct 3 separator bands (pages 26–27).

8. Sew the separator bands to 3 braid strips.

9. Sew the braid/separator band units together.

10. Construct and attach the borders (page 73).

11. Construct the backing; layer the top with the batting and backing (page 73). Quilting suggestions are on page 72.

12. Make the binding and bind (page 74).

8 Thanks, Frank

Stained and Braided

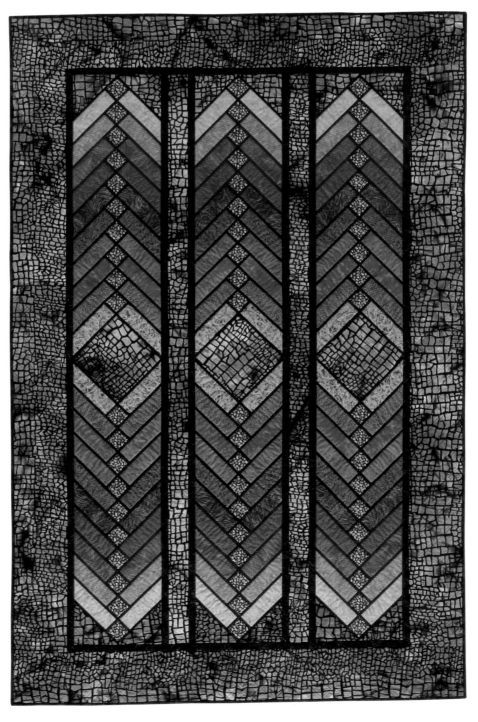

FINISHED SIZE: 46″ × 72″

Fabric Requirements

- ¼ yard each of 10 fabrics for braid run—fat quarters okay

- 1⅞ yards black for leading, separator band outline strips, inner borders, and binding

- ⅜ yard for accent squares

- 1⅞ yards nondirectional main fabric for center squares, ending triangles, separator band center strips, and outer borders

- 3 yards for backing if pieced crosswise (4½ yards if pieced lengthwise)

- 50″ × 76″ batting

Note ◆◆◆◆◆◆◆◆◆◆◆◆

Thanks, Frank requires careful piecing of the black fabric, but you might be able to obtain a similar effect by appliquéing black bias tape. Once you have constructed the segments, the strips are built as for any center-out braid.

Cutting

BRAIDS: From each fabric, cut one strip 7″ × width of fabric; then cut the strips into 2 rectangles 7″ × 13″. OR, from each fat quarter, cut 2 strips, from selvage to center, 7″ wide; then trim each to 13″.

BLACK FABRIC: Cut 19 strips ¾″ × length of fabric; from 2 of the strips, cut 10 pieces 13″ long. Cut 8 strips 1¼″ × length of fabric. The binding will be cut later from leftovers.

ACCENTS: Cut 4 strips 2″ × width of fabric; then cut each strip into thirds.

MAIN FABRIC: Cut the pieces in the order listed. Cut 4 strips 6″ wide and 2 strips 2″ wide, all by length of fabric. From the remaining fabric, cut 3 squares 6⅞″ × 6⅞″ and 6 squares 6½″ × 6½″. Cut each 6½″ square in half diagonally to obtain 12 half-square triangles.

Construction

Refer to Chapters 3 and 4, and pages 34–35 for basic instructions.

1. Separate the braid fabrics into 2 piles (page 13).

2. From one pile, cut 2 segments 2″ wide from each fabric. Audition the segments with the accent and center-square fabrics; rearrange or replace as needed (pages 14–15). Cut 4 more segments from each fabric in the first pile.

3. Sew a ¾″ × 13″ black strip to each fabric in the second pile of braid fabrics. Sew with the black fabric on top; press the seams toward the braid fabrics.

4. Sew a 13″ piece of accent fabric to the remaining side of each black fabric strip you sewed in Step 3. Sew with black on top and use a ¼″ foot and the previous seam as stitching guides. Press the seams toward the black fabric.

5. Cut into 6 segments 2″ wide from each fabric.

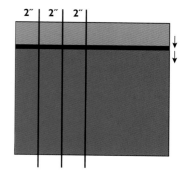

Sew and cut braid, black, and accent fabrics.

6. Lay a long ¾" black strip face up on the table. Place a segment from Step 2 on it face down. If your braid fabric is directional, the top of the motif should be closest to you. Sew; continue adding segments until all of them have been sewn to the black strip. Press the seams toward the segments.

7. Sew the segments from Step 5 similarly, except that the accent fabric end of the segment should now go through the machine first. Press the seams toward the segments.

Sew segments to black.

8. Use a ruler and rotary cutter to trim the black strips even with both ends of each segment.

9. Construct the braids using the center-out method (pages 34–35), adding a ¾" strip of black before attaching the ending triangles. Be careful to align the black fabric strips when you add the accented segments. Pinning on both sides of the black piece helps.

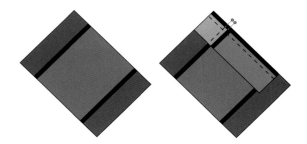

Align the black strips.

10. Mark the sides, trim the ends, and measure the braid lengths (page 25).

11. Construct the 2 separator bands (pages 26–27).

12. Sew the separator bands to 2 braid strips.

13. Sew the braid/separator units together.

14. Attach the borders (page 73).

15. Construct the backing; layer the top with batting and backing (page 73). Quilting suggestions are on page 72.

16. Make the binding and bind (page 74).

9

Mi Casa
Es Su Casa

FINISHED SIZE: 40″ × 53″

Quilted by Barbara Lacey

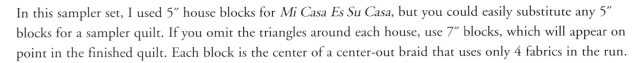

In this sampler set, I used 5″ house blocks for *Mi Casa Es Su Casa*, but you could easily substitute any 5″ blocks for a sampler quilt. If you omit the triangles around each house, use 7″ blocks, which will appear on point in the finished quilt. Each block is the center of a center-out braid that uses only 4 fabrics in the run.

Make the blocks first, then find the fabric for the surrounding triangles. Select the braid fabrics next. If you want a scrappy look, the fabrics should be similar in appearance within each color; that is, all the reds should be similar, as should all the greens, and so on. For best results, use at least 6 fabrics in each color. The accent fabric is selected last; you can avoid headaches by using something nondirectional.

Fabric Requirements

- Scraps to total about 1½ yards to make the houses

- ¾ yard nondirectional fabric for setting triangles and to surround houses

- Scraps of 6 to 8 fabrics to total ¼ yard in each of 4 color families OR ¼ yard each of 4 fabrics for braid run

- ⅛ yard for accent squares

- ¼ yard for inner borders

- 1⅜ yards for outer borders, cut lengthwise

- 1⅝ yards for backing

- ⅜ yard for binding

- 44″ × 57″ batting

Note ◆◆◆◆◆◆◆◆◆◆◆◆

If you want to use the same fabric for the setting triangles and borders, as I did, purchase 1⅜ yards for all. There is enough fabric for everything after you cut the borders lengthwise.

Cutting

Cut the house block pieces as directed below.

For each house block: (You will need to make 8 total):

Section	Piece	Number	Cut Size
Front	A/Door	1	2⅜″ × 1½″
Front	B/Lintel	1	1⅛″ × 1½″
Front	C/Front walls	2	3″ × 1″
Side	D/Window	1	1¾″ × 1½″
Side	E/Window sills	2	1⅛″ × 1½″
Side	F/Walls	2	3″ × 1½″
Roof	G/Gable	1	2½″ × 2⅞″
Roof	H/Roof	1	4⅞″ × 2¼″
Roof	I/Middle sky	2	3″ × 1¾″
Sky	J/Top sky	2	1¼″ × 2⅝″
Sky	K/Chimney	1	1¼″ × 1¼″

SUBCUTTING HOUSE BLOCK PIECES G, H, AND I: For piece G, use the 60° lines on your ruler to make 2 cuts, one in each direction, with a 2⅞″ side as the base; for piece H with the fabric right side up, cut 2 parallel 60° angles across the short ends of the rectangle; and for piece I, place the 2 rectangles right sides together; cut diagonally to obtain 2 sets of I and I-reversed triangles.

OR, use the template patterns on page 78 to cut one G, one H, one I, and one I-reversed.

HOUSE BLOCK TRIANGLES/SETTING TRIANGLES (SEE NOTE ABOVE): Cut 2 strips 4¾″ × width of fabric. Cut the strips into 16 squares 4¾″ × 4¾″; then cut the squares in half diagonally to obtain 32 half-square triangles. Cut 2 squares 11½″ × 11½″; then cut the squares in half diagonally twice to obtain 8 quarter-square triangles (you will use 6). Cut 2 squares 6½″ × 6½″; then cut the squares in half diagonally to make 4 half-square triangles.

BRAIDS: From scraps, cut 24 pieces, each 1½″ × 7¾″ from each color family OR, from yardage, cut one strip 7¾″ × width of fabric from each fabric; then cut the strips in half.

ACCENTS: Cut 2 strips 1½″ × width of fabric.

INNER BORDERS: Cut 4 strips 1½″ × width of fabric.

OUTER BORDERS: Cut 4 strips 4½″ × length of fabric.

Construction

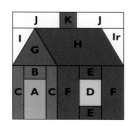

House block

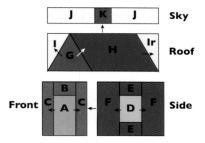

House block assembly

1. **Front:** Sew A to B; press the seam in either direction. Sew one piece C to each side of the AB unit; press the seams toward the C pieces.

2. **Side:** Sew one piece E to each short side of piece D; press the seams in either direction. Sew one piece F to each side of the DE unit; press the seams toward the F pieces.

3. **Roof:** Sew G to H; press the seam toward H. Sew piece I to one end of the GH unit; sew the I-reversed piece to the other end. Press the seams toward the I pieces.

4. **Sky:** Sew one piece J to each side of piece K; press the seams in either direction.

5. **Building:** Sew the front (ABC) unit to the side (DEF) unit; press the seam toward the ABC unit. Sew the sky (JK) unit to the roof (GHI) unit; press the seam toward the sky. Sew the 2 block halves together, making sure that the GH and CF seams match at the ¼″ seam-line. Press.

6. Sew the long side of a 4¾″ triangle to each side of each house block. The triangles will be bigger than the blocks, so match the approximate centers as you sew. Press the seams toward the triangles.

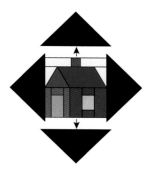

Sew triangles to block.

7. Use a square ruler to cut the house blocks down to 7⅝″ squares.

8A. If using yardage for the braids, separate the pieces into 2 piles (page 13). From one pile, cut 2 segments 1½″ wide from each fabric. Lay these out with the accent fabric and a house block; rearrange or replace as needed. Cut 10 more segments from each fabric in the first pile.

9A. Cut the accent strips in half at the center fold. Sew an accent strip to each fabric in the second pile of braid strip fabrics. Subcut the fabric pairs into 12 segments 1½″ wide each.

8B. If using scraps for the braids, lay out a few with the accent fabric and house blocks; decide on the order of the color families.

9B. Subcut the accent strips into 48 squares 1½″ × 1½″. Sew one square to each end of 12 braid segments in each color family.

10. Construct 6 braids using the center-out method, with the 6 house blocks as the center squares (pages 34–35).

11. Trim the sides of the braids (pages 17–18) and staystitch the bias edges.

Construct 6.

12. Lay out the 6 braid strips, the 2 remaining house blocks, and 6 triangles 11½″ wide to determine placement.

13. Sew the braids, the house blocks, and 2 of the 11½″ triangles together, following the order in the diagrams below. Match the seamlines and press the seams in the direction of the arrows. Make sure all the house roofs are pointing the same direction, and pin at every braid seam. Seams 8, 10, 12, and 13 are Y-seams. Mark dots at each seam intersection, ¼″ from the cut edge. You will start stitching, stop stitching, and backstitch at each dot.

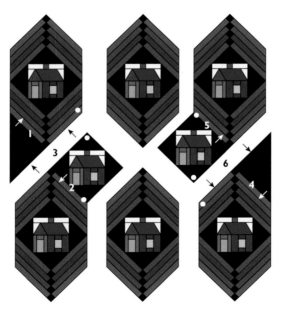

Attach side triangles and 2 house blocks. Stop stitching and backstitch at seamline (shown by dots).

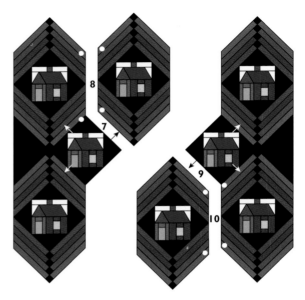

Attach remaining 2 house braids.

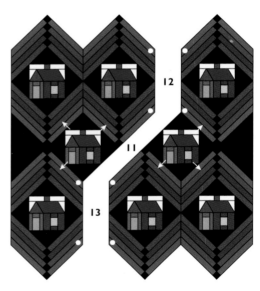

Final seams. Stop stitching and backstitch at dots.

14. Sew four 11½″ triangles into the V's at the ends of the braids using Y-seams.

15. Sew a 6½″ triangle onto each corner and trim to square the quilt.

16. Construct and attach the borders (page 73).

17. Layer the top with batting and backing (page 73). Quilting suggestions are on page 72.

18. Make the binding and bind (page 74).

6 Adding Separator Band Variations

In this chapter, we will alter only the separator bands; the construction of the braid strips remains as in the preceding chapters. Read the instructions in advance, and buy extra braid fabric if you even suspect you may try pieced separators.

Simple Pieced Separator Bands

The simplest pieced separator band is made up of rectangles pieced from the same fabrics and in the same order as the braid strips (or in reverse order). If you examine the separators in *Lava Lamp* (page 52) closely, you will see that every fabric in the center separator appears twice. The resulting larger purple area in the center offsets the large green center squares, but you may prefer a single center rectangle. Be careful, because your choice will affect the math.

Cutting and Construction

1. To determine the cutting width for center-rectangle strips, first find the finished length of your braid strips (pages 25–26), usually about 79″ for a twelve-fabric braid variation. Divide this number by the total number of rectangles, not the number of fabrics, that you will use in each band, 24 in this example: 79″ ÷ 24 = 3.29″. (If you had decided to use the center fabric only once, you would divide by 23.) Adding ½″ to this number for seam allowances gives 3.79″. This measurement is the cutting width for the strips, but it needs some adjusting. Since 3.79″ is just over 3¾″, it is tempting to cut there. But if you do so, your center band will be too short. However, cutting 3⅞″ strips will make the center band too long. Use masking tape or Glow-Line tape to mark a line on your ruler that is between the 3¾″ and the 3⅞″ lines. The resulting finished band will still be

slightly too long (by ½″–1″), but it can be trimmed at both ends without a noticeable difference in the size of the end rectangles. From each braid fabric, cut one strip from selvage to selvage (or from selvage to center for fat quarters) that is the width you determined in Step 1.

2. Sew the strips together in the order of the braid run, matching the long raw edges. Press the seams toward the darker end. Handling the strips will be easier if you sew them together in pairs, then fours, and so on; and your seams will be straighter if you consistently keep either the odd- or even-numbered fabrics on top as they go through the machine. You will be alternating the ends of the strips to begin stitching.

3. Use your rotary cutter to trim one end even, cutting parallel to the selvages; then cut 6 strips 3½″ wide. Fold the unit parallel to the seams if necessary to fit it on your cutting mat.

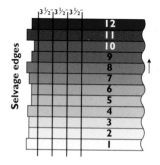

Subcutting for center separator band. Cut 6.

4. Sew pairs of the strips together at the middle fabric (purple in *Lava Lamp*, page 50) and use the resulting units as your center separator bands.

10

Lava Lamp

Separator Band from Rectangles

FINISHED SIZE: 70″ × 90″

Quilted by Barbara Lacey

Fabric Requirements

Purchase now

- ½ yard each of 12 fabrics for braid run and center separators—fat quarters okay
- ½ yard for accent squares—fat quarters okay
- ¼ yard for center squares (⅝ yard if directional)
- ½ yard nondirectional for ending triangles—fat quarters okay

Purchase later

- 1¼ yards for separator bands, outline strips
- ½ yard for inner borders
- 1¼ yards for outer borders (2⅜ yards if you prefer not to piece)
- 5½ yards for backing (pieced lengthwise)
- ⅝ yard for binding
- 74″ × 94″ batting

Cutting

Refer to Chapter 3 and 4, pages 34–35, and 49 for basic instructions.

BRAIDS: From each fabric, cut one strip 8½″ × width of fabric; then cut each strip in half. OR, from each fat quarter, cut 2 strips, from selvage to center, 8½″ wide.

ACCENTS: Cut 6 strips 2½″ × width of fabric; then cut the strips in half. OR, from fat quarters, cut 12 strips, from selvage to center, 2½″ wide.

CENTER SQUARES (PAGES 34–35): Cut 4 squares 8⅜″ × 8⅜″.

ENDING TRIANGLES: Cut 8 squares 7″ × 7″; then cut the squares in half diagonally to obtain 16 half-square triangles.

SEPARATOR BANDS, OUTLINE STRIPS (PAGE 26): Cut 12 strips 1½″ × length of fabric.

CENTER STRIPS (PAGE 49): From each braid fabric, cut one strip, determined dimension by the width of the fabric.

INNER BORDERS: Cut 8 strips 1½″ × width of fabric.

OUTER BORDERS: Cut 8 strips 5″ × length of fabric. OR, cut 4 strips 5″ × length of fabric if you have purchased enough for unpieced borders.

Construction

Refer to Chapter 3 and 4, pages 34–35, and 49 for basic instructions.

1. Construct 4 braids using the center-out method (pages 34–35).

2. Mark the sides, trim the ends, and measure the braids (page 25).

3. Cut and construct 3 center separator strips (page 49).

4. Construct the separator bands (pages 26–27).

5. Sew the separator bands to the 3 braid strips.

6. Sew the braid/separator band units together.

7. Construct and attach the borders (page 73).

8. Construct the backing; layer the top with the batting and backing (page 73). Quilting suggestions are on page 72.

9. Make the binding and bind (page 74).

French Braids as Separator Bands

Although using French braids as separator bands requires more cutting and sewing than bands made of simple rectangles, some quilters may prefer the former because the construction is familiar and the results are dramatic. The separators consist of the same fabrics as the braids, but because the separators are narrower, they do not extend to the top edge of the quilt. The usual ending triangles are replaced by endcaps, which are attached in one of three ways.

Varying the Location of the First Braid Fabric

Fabric Selection

Look carefully at *Shadow City* (page 54); the only new aspect of fabric selection is the addition of a second accent fabric. If you want the look of this particular quilt, the contrast between fabrics #1 and #12 in the braid run must be high.

Cutting and Construction

1. Construct the braid strips as for a basic braid (Chapter 3; and *Shadow City*, Steps 1 and 2, page 55).

2. Construct the braid separator bands as for basic braid strips, using the second accent fabric and braid strips that are cut 4″ × width of fabric; then cut in half (*Shadow City*, Cutting and Steps 3–5, pages 55–56).

3. Add endcaps to the end of each separator braid using one of the methods described below:

Method A. Endcaps made using oversize triangles: Sew an 8″ half-square triangle to one side of the separator. Press the seam toward the triangle and trim the tip of the triangle even with the braid edge. Sew a second 8″ half-square triangle to the other side of the separator. Press the seam toward the triangle. Proceed to Step 4.

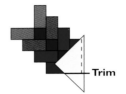

Stitch triangles to separator band.

Method B. Endcaps made using the 5″ × 7″ rectangles and a Y-seam: Construct 3 endcaps from the 3 rectangles cut from the ending triangle/endcap fabric. Fold with right sides together, matching the 5″ sides, and press. Use a ruler and rotary cutter to cut a 45° angle from one corner of the raw edge side across to the folded side. If your fabric is directional, cut up from the bottom of the motif. Find the point where the seamline on the 45° cut meets a line drawn ¼″ from the fold. Use a marker that doesn't show through to the front to mark dots on the wrong side of both sides where the 2 lines intersect. Match the dots and sew a ¼″ seam along the folded edge, stopping and backstitching at the dots. Now slice a tiny bit—about 2 threads—off the folded edge. These are your endcaps.

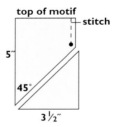

Cut and stitch endcaps.

Mark a dot at the top point of the braid where the 2 seamlines intersect. To attach the endcaps to the separators with a Y-seam, pin the left side of the endcap to the left side of the separator, matching the dot on the braid with the dot on the left side of the endcap. The edges are not the same length, so pin out from the top point of the braid. With the endcap on top, sew the seam from the outer edge toward the center, stopping and backstitching at the dot, and taking care not to stitch into the seam. Repeat for the right side, this time sewing from the endcap seam to the edge. Press these seams toward the endcap; then press the center seam to one side. Repeat for the other 2 separators.

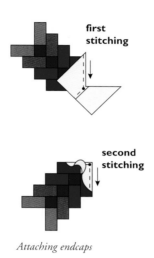

Attaching endcaps

Method C. Endcaps made using one 6″ × 7″ rectangle each: This method is similar to Method B but attaching the endcaps is more challenging. This method works well when you want to use a large print for the endcap fabric.

Cut a rectangle 6″ × 7″. Use a 45-45-90° triangle ruler to mark a V-cut on a 6″ side of the separator endcaps. Cut and remove the V-cut.

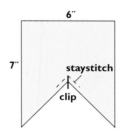

Endcap construction

To attach an endcap to a braid, first use small stitches to staystitch the V-cut *just inside* the stitching line (within the seam allowance) for about ½″ on each side of the V. Use the tips only of a sharp pair of scissors to snip the 90° angle of the V from the raw edge to the staystitching.

On the wrong side at the top point of the braid strip, make a dot where the seamlines intersect. Don't mark with something that shows through to the right side.

To attach the endcaps to the separators with a Y-seam, refer to the illustrations below Method B. Lay out the braid right side up; then place the endcap next to it as it will appear when finished. Flip the endcap over the left side of the top of the braid so the right sides are together and pin, first matching the inside point of the V-cut to the dot on the braid. Sew from the edge of the endcap to the turn in the V-cut stitching line; backstitch and remove the unit from the sewing machine. Pull the other side of the V-cut around so that the remaining raw edge is aligned with the other side of the braid strip. Pin as before. Stitch from the V-cut to the edge of the endcap, backstitching at the beginning of the seam. Smooth the endcap back from the braid; if you have sewn correctly, there should be no puckering at the V-cut, but a tiny pucker can often be pressed out. Press the seams toward the endcaps.

4. Mark the sides of the separators as for a braid strip; trim the starting triangle ends, but DO NOT trim the endcap ends. Add outline strips and trim dog ears.

5. When you have determined the universal length of the braid strips, trim each separator band to the desired length *at the endcap end only.*

11

Shadow City

Varying the First Braid Fabric

FINISHED SIZE: 79″ × 87″

Fabric Requirements

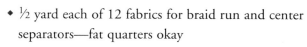

Purchase now

- ½ yard each of 12 fabrics for braid run and center separators—fat quarters okay
- ½ yard for accent #1 (braids)—fat quarters okay
- ½ yard for accent #2 (separators)—fat quarters okay
- ⅜ yard nondirectional fabric for starting triangles
- ½ yard nondirectional fabric for ending triangles and endcaps

Purchase later

- 1⅛ yards for separator bands outline strips
- ½ yard for inner borders
- 2¼ yards for outer borders
- 5¼ yards for backing (pieced lengthwise)
- ⅝ yard for binding
- 83″ × 91″ batting

Cutting

Refer to pages 13–15 for detailed instructions.

BRAIDS: From each fabric, cut one strip 8½″ × width of fabric; then cut the strips in half. OR, from each fat quarter, cut 2 strips, from selvage to center, 8½″ wide.

CENTER SEPARATORS: From each braid fabric, cut one strip 4″ × width of fabric; then cut the strips in half. OR, from each fat quarter, cut 2 strips from selvage to center 4″ wide.

ACCENT #1: Cut 6 strips 2½″ × width of fabric; then cut the strips in half. OR, from fat quarters, cut 12 strips, from selvage to center, 2½″ wide.

ACCENT #2: Cut 6 strips 2½″ × width of fabric; then cut the strips in half. OR, from fat quarters, cut 12 strips, from selvage to center, 2½″ wide.

STARTING TRIANGLES: Cut 4 quarter-square triangles, each with a 13″ base. Cut one 7″ × 7″ square; then cut the square in half diagonally twice to obtain 4 quarter-square triangles.

ENDING TRIANGLES/ENDCAPS: Cut 4 squares 7″ × 7″; then cut the squares in half diagonally to obtain 8 half-square triangles. For endcaps, refer to pages 52–53 and cut fabric to make 3 endcaps.

SEPARATOR BANDS, OUTLINE STRIPS (PAGE 26): Cut 12 strips 1½″ × length of fabric.

INNER BORDERS: Cut 8 strips 1½″ × width of fabric.

OUTER BORDERS: Cut 4 strips 6½″ × length of fabric.

Construction

Refer to Chapter 3 and 4, pages 34–35, and 52–53 for basic instructions.

1. Construct 4 basic braids (pages 16–17), using accent #1. Although the order of the braid fabrics is the same for all 4 braids, no 2 braids begin with the same fabric. The first braid follows the usual sequence of #1 through #12 and then repeat. The second braid starts with fabric #9, continues through #12, then #1 through #12, then #1 through #8. The third braid sequence is #5 through #12, #1 through #12, #1 through #4. The fourth braid sequence is #7 through #12, #1 through #12, #1 through #6.

2. Mark the sides, trim the ends, and measure the braid lengths (page 25).

3. In the separators, the braid fabric that begins the band reappears at the top, so each separator band uses one extra set of segments (25, not 24). Although the order of the braid fabrics remains the same for all the separators, no 2 separators begin with the same fabric.

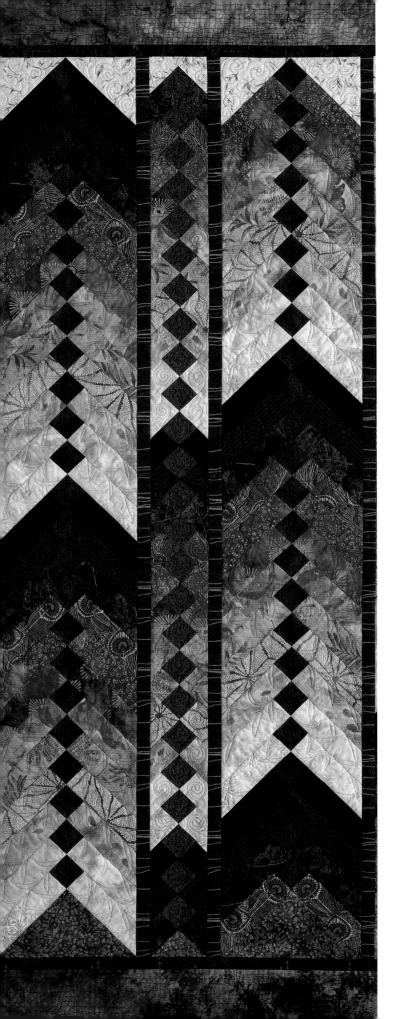

Begin one separator band with fabric #10 and continue through #12, then #1 through #12, then #1 through #10. The fabric sequence for the second separator is #6 through #12, #1 through #12, #1 through #6. The final separator sequence is #5 through #12, #1 through #12, #1 through #5.

4. Separate the fabrics for the center separator strip into 2 piles as for the braid strips. From one pile, cut 8 segments 2½″ wide from fabrics #5, #6, and #10; then cut 6 segments 2½″ wide from the other fabrics.

5. Sew a strip of accent #2 to each fabric in the second pile, as for braid strips. Subcut fabrics #5, #6, and #10 into 8 segments 2½″ wide. Subcut the other fabrics into 6 segments 2½″ wide.

6. Construct the center separator strips with endcaps (pages 52–53), using the fabric sequence from Step 3.

7. Mark the sides of the separator bands as you would for a basic braid, measuring out 2½″–2¾″ from the center (page 25), and attach the outline strips to construct 3 separator bands (pages 26–27).

8. Adjust the length of the separators and sew them to the 3 braid strips (pages 27 and 53).

9. Sew the braid/separator band units together.

10. Construct and attach the borders (page 73).

11. Construct the backing; layer the top with the batting and backing (page 73). Quilting suggestions are on page 72.

12. Make the binding and bind (page 74).

Separators Using Reverse Braid Order

Fabric Selection

The braid-run fabric selection for *Big Red* is more challenging than usual because the fabrics are restricted to one color family. You can use any color, but pick one that will contrast with the black-and-white accents. An easier version of this quilt could be made using a single accent fabric, or one accent fabric for the braid run and another for the separators.

When you have selected the braid-run fabrics, pick the accent fabrics. This is just like picking a braid run from black-and-white fabrics. Arrange the braid-run fabrics from light to dark; arrange the accent fabrics beside them from dark to light, pairing the lightest braid fabric with the darkest accent, the second lightest braid fabric with the second darkest accent, and so on, until the darkest braid fabric is assigned to the lightest accent. Each accent will appear with the same braid fabric throughout the quilt.

Cutting and Construction

The braid strip and separator band construction is the same as for any center-out braid (pages 34–35). The separator endcaps are cut as one piece to take advantage of the large black-and-white print. Because this makes attaching them more difficult, however, you may prefer to use a simpler endcap method (pages 52–53).

1. Construct the braid strips as for basic center-out braids (Chapter Five, pages 34–35; and *Big Red*, Cutting and Steps 1 and 2, page 61), matching the assigned accent to each braid fabric.

2. Construct the separator bands as basic center-out braids, cutting the braid fabrics 4″ wide, and again matching the accent fabrics. (*Big Red*, Steps 3–6, pages 59–60).

3. Add endcaps to both ends of the separator braids using one of the methods found on pages 52–53.

4. When you have attached all the endcaps, mark the sides of the separators as for a center-out braid strip (step 3, page 35).

5. Attach the outline strips. Once you find the universal length of your braid strips, these separator bands are treated as any others and trimmed at both ends.

12

Big Red

Using Reverse Braid Order

FINISHED SIZE: 76″ × 85″

Fabric Requirements

Purchase now

- ½ yard each of 11 fabrics for braid run and center separators—fat quarters okay

- ⅛ yard each of 11 fabrics for accent squares—fat eighths okay

- ½ yard nondirectional fabric for center braid squares and separator endcaps

- ½ yard nondirectional fabric for center separator squares and braid ending triangles

Purchase later

- 1¼ yards for separator bands, outline strips

- ½ yard for inner borders

- 1¼ yards for outer borders (2¼ yards if you prefer not to piece)

- 5⅛ yards for backing (pieced lengthwise)

- ⅝ yard for binding

- 80″ × 89″ batting

Cutting

BRAIDS: From each fabric, cut one strip 8½″ × width of fabric; then cut the strips in half. OR, from each fat quarter, cut 2 strips, from selvage to center, 8½″ wide.

CENTER SEPARATORS: From each braid fabric, cut one strip 4″ wide; then cut the strips in half. OR, from each fat quarter, cut 2 strips, from selvage to center, 4″ wide.

ACCENTS: From each accent fabric, cut 1 strip 2½″ × width of fabric; then cut the strips in half. OR, from each fat quarter, cut 2 strips, from selvage to center, 2½″ wide.

CENTER BRAID SQUARES/SEPARATOR ENDCAPS: Cut one strip 8⅜″ × width of fabric; subcut the strip into 4 squares 8⅜″ × 8⅜″. For endcaps, refer to pages 52–53. and cut fabric to make 6 endcaps.

CENTER SEPARATOR SQUARES/BRAID ENDING TRIANGLES: Cut 2 strips 7″ × width of fabric. Cut 8 squares 7″ × 7″; then cut the squares in half diagonally to obtain 16 half-square triangles. Trim the remainder of the 7″ strips down to 3⅞″; subcut the strips into 3 squares 3⅞″ × 3⅞″.

SEPARATOR BANDS, OUTLINE STRIPS: Cut 12 strips 1½″ × length of fabric.

INNER BORDERS: Cut 8 strips 1½″ × width of fabric.

OUTER BORDERS: Cut 8 strips 5″ × length of fabric. OR, cut 4 strips 5″ × length of fabric if you have purchased enough for unpieced borders.

Construction

Refer to Chapters 3 and 4, pages 34–35, and 57 for basic instructions.

1. Construct 4 braids using the center-out method (pages 34–35), beginning with the darkest braid fabric.

2. Mark the sides, trim the ends, and measure the braid lengths (page 25).

3. Separate the fabrics for the center separator strips into 2 piles as for braid strips. From one pile, cut 6 segments 2½″ wide from each fabric.

4. Sew the remaining half strip of pre-assigned accent fabric to each fabric in the second pile of center-strip fabrics, as for braid strips. Subcut the fabric pairs into 6 segments 2½″ wide.

5. Construct 3 center separator strips using the center-out method (pages 34–35), beginning with the lightest fabric. Add endcaps to both ends (pages 52–53).

6. Mark the sides of the separator bands as you would for a basic braid, measuring out 2½″–2¾″ from the center (page 25). Attach the outline strips to construct 3 separator bands (pages 26–27).

7. Trim the separators to your universal length, measuring from the center out.

8. Sew the separator bands to 3 braid strips (pages 26–27).

9. Sew the braid/separator band units together.

10. Construct and attach the borders (page 73).

11. Construct the backing; layer top with the batting and backing (page 73). Quilting suggestions are on page 72.

12. Make the binding and bind (page 74).

Separator Bands that Align with the Braids

Until now, the separator band variations have existed independent of the braid strips. Only the centers, quarter points, and ends were required to match. In the next two projects, the seams in the separator bands must line up precisely with those in the braid strips, so some construction techniques have been changed.

Reconstructed French Braids as Separator Bands

Fabric Selection

The separators in the next project are still made up of braid segments and accent squares. However, the accent squares are pieced to give the illusion of smaller squares floating in the separators. The starting triangles for the separators have also been eliminated and replaced by units pieced from the ending triangle fabric and the same "floaters." Use a mottled or indistinct print to disguise the many seams there.

Cutting and Construction

1. Cut the center separator and accent #2 fabrics as instructed (*Café Ole*, page 64).

2. The accent units are pieced like Log Cabin block centers. Sew a 1½" strip of the ending triangle fabric to a 1½" strip of the accent fabric. Press the seam toward the accent. Subcut into 18 segments 1½" wide.

3. Lay a 1½" ending triangle strip right side up on the table. Place the 1½" segments from Step 2 face down on the strip, aligning the long edges. Sew all the segments to the 1½" ending triangle strips; press the seams toward the strips. Use a rotary cutter and ruler to cut the strips even with the ends of the segments to make 18 accent units with the ending triangle fabric.

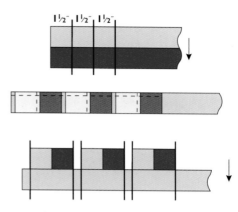

Constructing separator accent units

4. Make the same units using fabrics #2–#12 and the accent fabric. Cut a piece about 12" long from each 1½" strip of braid fabrics #2 through #12. Sew every 1½" × 12" braid fabric piece end to end onto 4 of the 1½" accent strips. Press all the seams toward the accent strips. Subcut each piece of braid/accent fabric into 6 segments 1½" wide.

5. Lay the remaining piece of each 1½" braid strip right side up on the table. Place the 6 segments from Step 4 face down on the strip, aligning the long edges; sew, press, and cut as in Step 3. Repeat for fabrics #3 through #12 to make 6 accent units from each of fabrics #2 through #12 of the braid run.

6. Sew one segment 2½" × 3½" to each accent unit, using the same braid fabric used in the accent unit and orienting every unit as shown in the illustration below. Press the seams toward the larger segments. You should now have 84 accent units, each with a 2½" × 3½" segment of its corresponding fabric sewn to one side. If you stack them with all the accent squares in the same position, the segments will all be on the same side.

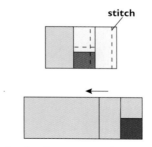

Sew braid segment to each accent unit.

7. Take the 6 units made from the ending triangle fabric and 6 unsewn 2½″ × 3½″ segments of the ending triangle fabric. Sew one accent unit to each segment. Then sew a second 2½″ × 3½″ segment of the ending triangle fabric to an adjacent side of the accent unit, making sure that it is oriented as illustrated. Repeat this process twice with the remaining ending triangle segments and accent units.

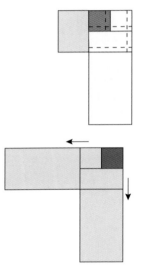

Begin the separator strips. Make 6.

8. The units from Step 7 will act as starting triangles for the separators, which are constructed as end-in braids (pages 38–39). Use the 5½″ quarter-square triangles as the center setting triangles.

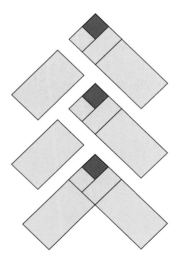

Separator braid construction

Installation

The seams in the braid strips and separators must line up when the top is finished. This alignment depends on the width of both the center strips and the outline strips.

1. Mark the sides of the braid strips as usual, trim the ends, and measure the length (page 25). Set the strips aside.

2. Trim the sides of the separator bands as you would for a basic braid without separators, measuring out 2¼″ from the center (pages 17–19). Do not trim the ends; staystitch the long edges within the seam allowances.

3. If you have sewn and cut accurately, your seams will align if you now add an outline strip approximately 1″ wide (finished). However, since seam allowances vary, check before cutting. Lay a braid strip on the table face up. Lay a separator next to it with the raw edge about ½″–1″ from the marked line. Problems in seam alignment must be adjusted at the midpoint, with the setting triangle seams, so start there. Move the separator nearer to and farther away from the braid strip until the seams of the setting triangles in the separators align with the seams between the first and second segments in the braid strip.

Aligning the braid strip and the separator

When you think that the alignment is correct, use a ruler to make sure that the seams are straight; then carefully measure the distance between the cut edge of the separator and the marked line on the braid strip.

Cut your outline strips to *this measurement plus 1″ (not ½″) in width*. Piece to obtain 6 strips of the necessary length. Cut these to the braid length.

4. Sew an outline strip to both sides of 2 braid strips (this is not the usual way of attaching separators), and sew an outline strip to one side of each of the 2 remaining braid strips. These outline strips are aligned with the marked braid strips and sewn exactly as if they were separator bands (page 27). Trim the dog ears as usual and press the seams toward the outline strips. Note that if there is an up and down to your braids, sew the last two outline strips so that you have braids for both sides of your quilt.

5. Find the center of the braid strips by folding across the points of the center squares; mark the centers on both outline strips in the outer seam allowance.

6. Lay out a braid strip on the table. Lay the edge of a ruler along the seamline between the second and third braid segments in the braid strip, extending it past the attached outline strip. Make a small pencil mark in the seam allowance without crossing the seamline. Mark the outline strips similarly at every second seamline.

Marking the outline strips

7. Find the center of the separator band by folding it where the 2 center accents meet. Pin the center to the midpoint of the outline strip, right sides together. Working from the back of the outline strip, with the outline/braid unit on top, find the first mark in the seam allowance and poke a pin through it exactly where it would intersect the ¼″ seam allowance.

8. With the pin still in place, poke the pin through the separator band at the seam between the second and third fabrics exactly where the seam intersects the ¼″ seamline. Pin the separator and braid strips together at this point. Continue aligning the other marks with their respective seamlines until you have matched all the marks in both directions from the center. Lay out the unit with the outline strips on top. The separator, which has not been trimmed, will be longer than the braid/outline unit; smooth the separator out flat, pin the layers together at the top of the braid strip, and let the rest of the separator extend past the top of the braid.

9. Sew the seam. Repeat for the 2 other braid strips, sewing all 3 separators to the same (left or right) side.

10. Press the seams toward the outline strip and trim the ends of the separators even with the braid/outline unit. Using a ruler to make sure that your trimmed end is at right angles to the seam. Staystitch across the ends of the separators. Sew these units into pairs and finish the top.

13 Café Ole

Reconstructed French Braids as Separator Bands

FINISHED SIZE: 74″ × 90″

Fabric Requirements

Purchase now

- ½ yard each of 12 fabrics for braid run and center separators
- ½ yard for accent #1 for braids—fat quarters okay
- ⅜ yard for accent #2 for separators
- ¼ yard for center squares (⅝ yard if directional)
- 1 yard nondirectional fabric for ending triangles and separator starters

Purchase later

- 1¼ yards for separator bands, outline strips
- ½ yard for inner borders
- 1¼ yards for outer borders (2⅜ yards if you prefer not to piece)
- 5⅜ yards for backing (pieced lengthwise)
- ⅝ yard for binding
- 78″ × 94″ batting

Cutting

Refer to pages 13–15 for basic instructions.

BRAIDS: From each fabric, cut one strip 8½″ × width of fabric; then cut the strips in half.

CENTER SEPARATORS: From fabric #1 of the braid run, cut 2 squares 5½″ × 5½″; then cut the squares in half diagonally twice to yield 8 quarter-square triangles (you will use 6). From fabrics #2 through #12 of the braid run, cut one strip 3½″ wide and one strip 1½″ wide, all by width of fabric. Subcut each 3½″ strip into 12 segments 2½″ wide.

ACCENT #1 (BRAIDS): Cut 6 strips 2½″ × width of fabric; then cut the strips in half. OR, from fat quarters, cut 12 strips, from selvage to center, 2½″ wide.

CENTER SQUARES (PAGE 34): Cut 4 squares 8⅜″ × 8⅜″.

ENDING TRIANGLES/SEPARATOR STARTERS: Cut 8 squares 7″ × 7″; then cut the squares in half diagonally to obtain 16 half-square triangles. Cut 3 strips 3½″ and 3 strips 1½″, all by width of fabric. Subcut the 3½″ strips into 36 segments 2½″ long.

ACCENT #2 (SEPARATORS): Cut 5 strips 1½″ × width of fabric.

SEPARATOR BANDS, OUTLINE STRIPS: Cut 12 length-wise strips, cutting width to be determined during construction.

INNER BORDERS: Cut 8 strips 1½″ × width of fabric.

OUTER BORDERS: Cut 8 strips 5″ × length of fabric. OR, cut 4 strips 5″ × length of fabric if you have purchased enough for unpieced borders.

Construction

Refer to Chapters 3 and 4, pages 34–35, and 61–63 for basic instructions.

1. Construct 4 braids using the center-out method (pages 34–35).

2. Mark the sides and trim the ends of the braids (page 25).

3. Construct 3 center separator strips and trim the sides of the strips (pages 34–35).

4. Determine the width of the outline strips, and cut and sew them to the braids (pages 62–63).

5. Sew the center strip units to 3 braid strips (Steps 5-9, page 63).

6. Sew the braid/separator strip units together (Step 10, page 63).

7. Construct and attach the border (page 73).

8. Construct the backing; layer the top with the batting and backing (page 73). Quilting suggestions are on page 72.

9. Make the binding and bind (page 74).

Chevron Separator Bands

Fabric Selection

The chevron separator band variation also requires aligning the seams in the separators with the seams in the braids. Nondirectional fabrics work best, especially for the center setting triangles.

Cutting and Construction

1. Cut strips from braid fabrics and center the setting triangle fabric as instructed (*Am I Blue?* page 68).

2. Separate the 2½" strips from the braid fabrics into 2 piles, each with one strip of each fabric. Work with one pile at a time.

3. Place fabrics #1 and #2 right sides together with fabric #2 on top and the end of fabric #2 about 2" down from the end of fabric #1; align the long edges and sew.

Sewing strips for chevrons

4. Continue adding strips in order, stairstepping as you go. You will be cutting at an angle, which is easier if you sew the strips into 2 groups of 6 each. Press all the seams toward the darker fabrics.

5. Repeat the process with the other pile of strips. However, this time rather than moving fabric #2 down, slide it up about 2", so it covers the top of fabric #1. Align the long edges and sew. Repeat for fabrics #3 through #12 and press all the seams toward the lighter fabrics. You have 2 sets of 12 strips each (or 4 sets of 6 each); the sets lean in opposite directions (see Step 6).

6. Align the 45° line on your ruler with a seamline to trim the stairstep ends off the strip sets. Cut 8 segments 1½" wide from each strip set.

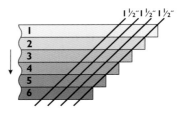

Cutting for chevrons. Cut 8 segments each.

7. If you have divided the strips into 4 sets, seam fabrics #6 and #7 of the corresponding sets, offsetting them as you would when joining bias-binding pieces. Sew; press the seams in the same direction as the other seams in the unit.

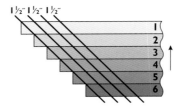

Sew chevron sets into longer pieces.

8. You now have 16 units, each comprising one piece each of fabrics #1 through #12. Eight lean in one direction and have seam allowances pressed toward the darker fabrics; the other 8 lean in the opposite direction and have seam allowances pressed toward the lighter end.

Place the long sides of one of each type of strip right sides together, with fabric #1 at the top. Butt the seamlines along the long raw edges, pin every seam, and sew from the seamline (¼" in from the edge) of fabric #1 to the edge of the other end of the strip.

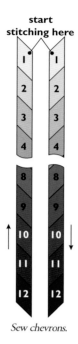

start stitching here

Sew chevrons.

9. Staystitch the remaining unsewn long edges within the seam allowances; then press the seam in either direction. Repeat this process 5 more times to make 6 chevrons. You will have 4 long chevron pieces left over, 2 of each type. Staystitch both the long bias edges of each piece.

10. From the 2½″ strips of fabric for the center setting triangles, cut 3 segments 15⅜″ long for the starting pieces for your 3 center separators. Use the 45° angle on your ruler to trim the ends to points to form elongated hexagons. This may be easier if you first fold the piece in half lengthwise.

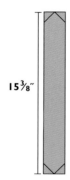

15⅜″

Trim ends of interior separator centers.

11. From the 1½″ strip, cut 2 segments 15⅞″ long. These will be the starting pieces for your outer separators. Place the 2 segments wrong sides together and use the 45° angle on your ruler to trim the ends in opposite directions. You should have 2 trapezoids that are mirror images.

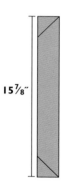

15⅞″

Trim ends of outer separator centers.

12. Attach a stitched chevron unit to both V-points of each of the 3 elongated hexagons from Step 10 by marking dots ¼″ from the V-points and sewing a Y-seam (pages 52–53). You will have 3 chevron strips; these are your center separators.

13. Sort the remaining chevron pieces into 2 pairs, each with one strip of each type (leaning left and leaning right). Sew the fabric #1 ends of each pair onto the ends of the trapezoid shapes from Step 11, just as you sewed the chevron sets together (page 66, Step 8). You now have 2 strips that are mirror-image half-chevrons. These pieces are the inner pieced vertical borders.

Installation

The center separators are attached to the braid strips in the same manner as for *Café Ole*, except that the midpoint of the separator is found by folding the hexagon so that its end points meet. (See pages 62–63, ignoring references to accent fabrics in the separators.) Trim the separator ends to the universal length of the braid strips, measuring from the center out.

The outer strips are attached using the same method: sew the outline strip to the braids, mark the outline strip, and match the seamlines to the half-chevrons.

Am I Blue?

Chevron Separator Bands

FINISHED SIZE: 69″ × 90″

Fabric Requirements

Purchase now

- ½ yard each of 12 fabrics for braid run and center separators
- ½ yard for accent squares—fat quarters okay
- ½ yard nondirectional fabric for starting triangles
- ¾ yard for center setting triangles and separator-centers

Purchase later

- 1¼ yards for separator bands, outline strips and inner borders
- 1¼ yards for outer borders (2⅜ yards if you prefer not to piece)
- 5⅜ yards for backing (pieced lengthwise)
- ⅝ yard for binding
- 73″ × 94″ batting

Cutting

BRAIDS: From each fabric, cut one strip 8½″ × width of fabric; then cut the strips in half.

CENTER SEPARATORS: From each braid fabric, cut 2 strips, 2½″ × width of fabric.

ACCENTS: Cut 6 strips 2½″ × width of fabric; then cut the strips in half. OR, from fat quarters, cut 12 strips, from selvage to center, 2½″ wide.

STARTING TRIANGLES: Cut 8 quarter-square triangles, each with a 13″ base.

CENTER SETTING TRIANGLES/SEPARATOR CENTERS: Cut 8 triangles as for the starting triangles. Cut 2 strips 2½″ wide and one strip 1½″ wide, all by width of fabric.

SEPARATOR BANDS, OUTLINE STRIPS/INNER BORDERS: Cut 24 strips 1¼″ × length of fabric.

OUTER BORDERS: Cut 8 strips 5″ × length of fabric. OR, cut 4 strips 5″ × length of fabric if you have purchased enough for unpieced borders.

Construction

Refer to Chapters 3 and 4, pages 38–39 and 66–67 for basic instructions.

1. Construct 4 braids using the end-in method (pages 38–39).

2. Mark the sides, trim the ends, and measure the lengths of the braids (page 25).

3. Construct 3 chevron center strips and 2 half-chevron outer strips (pages 66–67).

4. Trim the center separators to a universal length.

5. Attach the braids and separators, following Steps 4–8 for Reconstructed French Braids (pages 61–62). Ignore the references in Step 7 to finding the centers and remember in Step 8 that you have already trimmed your separator to the correct length.

6. Construct and attach the borders (page 73).

7. Construct the backing; layer top with batting and backing (page 73). Quilting suggestions are on page 72.

8. Make the binding and bind (page 74)

7 Adjusting the Size

Adjusting the Width

There are several ways to change the width of your quilt top. You can increase the total number of braid strips, increase the width of each strip, add extra separator bands, or use a combination of methods. An increase in the number of braid strips entails an increase in the number of separator bands. For example, rather than using 4 braid strips, you might use 5 or 6 for a larger quilt, which would necessitate 4 or 5 separators. If you still need just a few more inches, adding separator bands to the outer edges of the quilt before attaching the borders can be quite effective. (See *Am I Blue?* pages 68–69, where half-separators were added to the sides.)

There are also several ways to increase the width of the individual components. The simplest method is to increase the width of the separators, but if you increase the width too much, the braid strips will be lost. If you increase the width of the braid-fabric strips, you can also increase the width of the separators. To increase the finished width of each braid by over an inch (to about 12½″), change the original 8½″ cut for the braid fabrics to 9½″.

To decrease the width, reverse these processes: use fewer braid strips and separators or decrease the width of the braid strips or separators. In *Baby Braid* (pages 32–33), both these techniques were used.

Adjusting the Length

There are two ways to change the length. If you need just a few inches, the easiest lengthener is an increase in the number of fabrics in the braid run. Although sizes vary owing to individual seam allowances, adding one fabric to a two-run basic braid strip will increase the length by almost 6″. So by increasing the number of fabrics in the braid strip from 10 to 12, the you will increase the overall length from 62″ to about 73″.

If you need to add more than this, consider an extra run in each braid. Three runs of 10 (30 braid segments per strip) should yield a braid length of about 91″, which, with borders, should be long enough for almost any bed. You could also decrease the run to 9 fabrics, repeat it 3 times and use 27 segments (82″). Or, you could use 2 runs of 14 (or 4 runs of 7) for 28 segments (85″). There are many options. Remember, first determine the total number of segments you need in each braid; then decide on possible combinations.

Using the Tables

Assume that you want a quilt for your queen-sized bed. Measure to determine the desired size of your finished quilt. Let's say that you decide that you want your quilt to finish 90″ × 105″.

Because you must work with the dimensions of the pieced area, subtract the width of the borders from the finished size. This is an estimate, but on a quilt this size, 1″ inner and 6″ outer borders would be reasonable. Subtract 2″ for 2 inner borders and 12″ for 2 outer borders, for a total of 14″ from each dimension: the braided area should finish about 76″ × 91″.

To work with the width, go to Table 1 (page 71). Look at the center column. These are the approximate finished widths of the braid strips. For a quilt this size, you might go with a 12½″ finished strip. If you use 6 of these, you'll have 75″ (6 strips × 12½″) in width: wide enough, even without separator bands.

If you prefer separator bands, use 5 braid strips, for a total width of 62½″ (5 strips × 12½″). Look across to the left-hand column of the table to find the cut width of your braid-fabric strips; write down this width, because you will use it again later to determine the length.

To decide on the width of your separator bands, subtract the 62½" from your desired pieced width of 76" to get 13½". Divide this number by the number of separator bands (4 for 5 braids); your result is about 3⅜". This is not an easy number to work with; since the separator bands are often 4" (1" outline strip + 2" center strip + 1" outline strip), use that size for a total separator width of 16". This means the finished width of your pieced area will be 78½" (62½" + 16"). Close enough. (You could also decrease the center strip to 1½", for a finished separator of 3½".)

To figure the length, you must first decide whether your braid strips will be the original style, with starting and ending triangles, or a variation. Start with the desired finished length, 91". Go to Table 2. Use your format and the cut strip width from the previous step to determine how much of the length will be taken up by the starting triangles or squares. If you're using a basic braid format and a 9½" strip cut, you would subtract 6¼" (the amount added by the starting triangles) from your 91" length to end up with 84¾".

To find the number of 2" finished segments you would need per braid to obtain 84¾" in braid length, go to Table 3. Look down the right-hand column until you find a number close to yours, 84⅞" in this case. Then look across to the left-hand column to find the number of braid segments you need for each braid strip, 30 in this case. Thirty is a convenient number because it gives you many options: you could use 3 runs of 10, probably the best choice; or, if you were able to pick a 15-fabric braid run, you could obtain the same length with 2 runs. If you couldn't find the 10 fabrics you need, you could also use 5 runs of 6, or even 6 runs of 5. Just remember, this is the total number of segments for each braid strip, not for the entire quilt.

Table 1: Width

Cut width of braid-fabric strips	Approximate finished width of braid strip	Suggested finished width of separator band
6½"	8¼"	1"–2"
7½"	9¾"	2"–3"
8½"	11"	3"–4"
9½"	12½"	4"–5"

Table 2: Length

Cut width of braid-fabric strips	For basic braid: add approximately this much to length from Table 3	For variations: add approximately this much to length from Table 3
6½"	4¼"	8¼"
7½"	4¾"	9¾"
8½"	5½"	11"
9½"	6¼"	12½"

Table 3: Length

Number of 2½" (cut) segments per braid strip	Approximate finished length of braid strip
20	56½"
21	59⅜"
22	62¼"
23	65"
24	67⅞"
25	70¾"
26	73½"
27	76⅜"
28	79¼"
29	82"
30	84⅞"
31	87⅝"
32	90½"
33	93⅜"
34	96⅛"
35	99"
36	101¾"

Note ◆◆◆◆◆◆◆◆◆◆

If the final number of segments per braid is a number that can't be divided by other numbers, add or subtract a segment. If you are making a center-out or end-in braid, the total number of segments per braid must be an even number.

8 Finishing

Because of the frequent seams and lack of large empty spaces in French braid quilts, they are good candidates for machine quilting. I usually use cotton thread. First stabilize and separate the quilt into smaller sections by quilting in the ditch around the inside of the inner borders, in the ditches between the separator bands and the braid strips, and between the outline and center separator strips. Quilts without separators can be quilted in the ditch between the braid strips.

For the more visible areas, I change to a more noticeable thread and often stitch down the row of accent squares, either in a straight line with a walking foot or freehand using a simple decorative motif. The quilt is now divided into vertical sections, in which an overall, continuous design works well. The center strips of the separators can be quilted using the same motif or another, or even with a straight line down the center.

If you are not comfortable with freehand quilting, try quilting in the ditch up and down the braid segments across the quilt. This is easiest on a quilt without separator bands but can also be done by continuing the quilting line into the separators to their midpoints, then pivoting and continuing into the next braid strip (*Thanks, Frank*, pages 42–44). Draw or stitch a line down the center of each separator so you will know when to turn.

Another option is to treat individual segments as separate entities and quilt with a recurring motif. This takes a bit more skill and time than an overall pattern, so if you are nervous about your machine-quilting ability, avoid a high contrast between the fabric and the quilting thread. Invisible thread really does show less, as does thread in a color that matches the fabric. The latter option might mean using 2 or 3 colors of thread as you work your way up the braid strips (*Shadow City*, pages 54–55).

I often use an overall design for center squares and triangles and sometimes for the borders, but straight or wavy lines can also be used with good effect (*Thanks, Frank*, pages 42–44, and *Baby Braid*, pages 32–33). As with any quilting design, the choices are endless.

When selecting the binding fabric, first check for extra fabric from your outline strip, accent, and inner border fabrics. If you want a subtler binding, try using the border fabric itself. Whatever you pick, remember that if you want a quilt with visual impact, this is your last chance.

9 Quilting Basics

To make the quilt tops in this book, you need several beginning-level quilting skills: the ability to follow directions, cut with a rotary cutter, and sew an accurate ¼″ seam.

Specific instructions for the quilt tops are provided in the text; the following instructions will help you complete the quilt.

Butted Borders

The inner top and bottom borders of the quilts in this book are added first, then the side inner borders; however, the directions here are for adding the side borders first.

The side borders are usually attached first. When you have finished the quilt top, measure it vertically through the center. Cut the side borders to that length. Place pins at the centers of the two long sides of the quilt top and at the center of each side border strip. Pin the side borders to the quilt top, matching the center pins and the ends. Pin carefully and use a ¼″ seam allowance to sew the borders to the quilt top. Press the seams toward the border.

Measure horizontally across the center of the quilt top, including the side borders. Cut the top and bottom borders that length. Pin, sew, and press as above. Repeat the entire process for each set of borders.

Backing

Your backing should be a minimum of 2″ larger than the quilt top on all sides. You can purchase new fabric or piece the backing from any leftovers, but be sure to pre-wash new fabric and trim the selvages before you piece.

Batting

The type of batting to use depends on the desired look and the type of quilting you will do, but the batting should be cut approximately 2″ larger on all sides than your quilt top. If you are unfamiliar with the properties of various battings, ask at your local quilt shop.

Layering

Spread the backing wrong side up and tape down the edges with masking tape. (If your quilt is larger than your table, start with the center and work in sections, moving the quilt as needed.) Center the batting on top, smoothing out folds and patting down bulges. Place the quilt top right side up on top of the batting and backing, making sure it's centered.

Basting

If you plan to machine quilt, pin baste the quilt layers together with safety pins placed a minimum of 3″–4″ apart. Pin evenly over the entire surface of the quilt.

If you plan to hand quilt, baste the layers together with thread using a long needle (such as a 3½″ doll needle) and light-colored thread. Knot one end of the thread and use stitches 2″–3″ long. Begin at the center and move outward toward the edges, stitching parallel to the edges in rows 4″–6″ apart. When you have basted the layers thoroughly, baste around the edge of the quilt within the outer seam allowance, using stitches about ½″ long.

Binding

Double-Fold Straight-Grain or Bias Binding (French Fold)

1. Trim excess batting and backing from the quilt.

2. If you want a ¼" finished binding, cut the strips 2"–2¼" wide and piece them together with a diagonal seam to make a continuous binding strip.

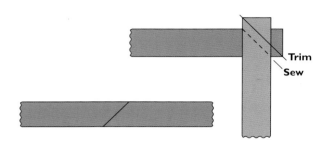

3. Press the seams open, then press the entire strip in half lengthwise with wrong sides together.

4. With raw edges even, pin the binding to the edge starting in the middle of one side, leaving about 6" of the binding unattached. Sew the binding to the quilt, using a ¼" seam allowance.

5. Stop ¼" away from the first corner and backstitch one stitch. Lift the presser foot and needle. Rotate the quilt one quarter turn.

Step 5. Stitch to ¼" from corner.

6. Fold the binding at a right angle so it extends straight above the quilt.

7. Then fold down the binding strip even with the top edge of the quilt.

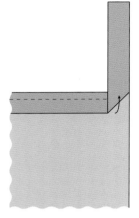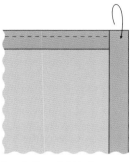

Step 6. First fold for miter

Step 7. Second fold alignment. Repeat in the same manner at all corners.

8. Begin sewing at the folded edge, backstitching at the beginning edge. Continue until you are 10"–12" away from the beginning binding stitches.

9. Pin the beginning unattached 6" of binding to the quilt by opening it out and pinning it at the fold, matching the raw edge to the raw edge of the quilt. Cut the other end (the last one you sewed on) so that it overlaps the pinned end by about 4".

10. Lay the cut end inside the pinned end. Mark the cut end on both edges where it meets the cut end; on the wrong side of the fabric, draw a faint line connecting the marks.

11. Cut that end of the binding ½" (not ¼") longer than the marked line, then sew the two binding ends together, placing the pieces at right angles to sew on the diagonal.

12. Finger-press the seam open and refold the binding as if it were one piece.

13. Realign all raw edges, pin the binding to the quilt, and stitch it down.

14. To finish the binding, flip the folded edge over to the back and whipstitch it in place by hand.

Last, don't forget to label your quilt, including at least your name and the year. A quilt name and city are also nice.

Appendix: Yardage and Cutting Charts

Yardage measurements in the following charts were rounded up to the nearest eighth yard, which in some cases is the absolute minimum required. Consider purchasing extra fabric when available.

Yardage—Basic Braid

All yardages are based on nondirectional fabrics and 40″ of useable width. All separators except crib size are cut lengthwise. FQ = fat quarter.

Size without borders (w × l)	Each braid fabric	Accent	Starting triangles	Ending triangles	Single separator	2-fabric separator— outline strips	2-fabric separator— center strip
Crib 27″ × 34″	¼ yd of 7 fabrics or 1 FQ each	¼ yd or FQ	¼ yd or FQ	¼ yd or FQ	¼ yd (cut crosswise)	n/a	n/a
Lap 44″ × 62″	¼ yd of 10 fabrics or 1 FQ each	½ yd or 2 FQs	¼ yd or FQ	¼ yd or FQ	n/a	n/a	n/a
Twin 56″ × 73″	¼ yd of 12 fabrics or 1 FQ each	½ yd or 2 FQs	¼ yd or FQ	¼ yd or FQ	1⅛ yd (pieced)	1⅛ yd (pieced)	1⅛ yd (pieced)
Queen 78½″ × 85½″	⅝ yd of 14 fabrics or ⅞ yd of 7 fabrics	1⅛ yd or ⅞ yd	½ yd	¼ yd	1¼ yd (pieced)	1¼ yd (pieced)	1¼ yd (pieced)
King 86″ × 85″	⅝ yd of 14 fabrics or ⅞ yd of 7 fabrics	1⅛ yd or ⅞ yd	½ yd	½ yd	2½ yd (not pieced)	1¼ yd (pieced)	1¼ yd (pieced)

Yardage—Braid Variations

Yardages for braid and accent fabrics are the same as for the original braid. All yardages are based on nondirectional fabrics and 40″ of useable width. All separators except crib size are cut lengthwise. FQ = fat quarter.

Size without borders (w × l)	CENTER-OUT		END-IN		CENTER-OUT or END-IN		
	Center triangles	Ending Triangles	Starting Triangles	Center Triangles	Single separator	2-Fabric separator —outline strips	2-Fabric separator —center strips
Crib 27″ × 38″	¼ yd or FQ	¼ yd or FQ	¼ yd	¼ yd or FQ	¼ yd (cut crosswise)	n/a	n/a
Lap 44″ × 67″	¼ yd or FQ	½ yd	½ yd	½ yd	n/a	n/a	n/a
Twin 56″ × 79″	¼ yd or FQ	½ yd	½ yd	½ yd	1¼ yd (pieced)	1¼ yd (pieced)	1¼ yd (pieced)
Queen 78½″ × 92″	⅝ yd	½ yd	⅝ yd	⅝ yd	1⅜ yd (pieced)	1⅜ yd (pieced)	1⅜ yd (pieced)
King 86″ × 90″	⅝ yd	¾ yd	¾ yd	¾ yd	2⅝ yd (not pieced)	1⅜ yd (pieced)	1⅜ yd (pieced)

Cutting—Braid Strips and Accents—All Styles

Numbers are based on 40″ of useable width. Dimensions in parentheses are for braid variations. Braid and accent fabrics are cut crosswise. All separators except crib size are cut lengthwise. FQ = fat quarter.

Size without borders (w × l)	Number of braid strips	Number of fabrics in braid run	Braid runs per braid strip	Cut from *each* braid fabric	Cut from accent fabric	Segments from *each* braid fabric
Crib (with 1″ separator bands) 27″ × 34″ (27″ × 38″)	3	7	2	1 strip 6½″	4 strips 2″ or 8 strips 2″ from FQs	Cut 2″ wide; 6 with accent, 6 without
Lap (with no separator bands) 44″ × 62″ (44″ × 67″)	4	10	2	1 strip 8½″	5 strips 2½″ or 10 strips 2″ from FQs	Cut 2½″ wide; 8 with accent, 8 without
Twin (with 4″ separator bands) 56″ × 73″ (56″ × 79″)	4	12	2	1 strip 8½″	6 strips 2½″ or 12 strips 2½″ from FQs	Cut 2½″ wide; 8 with accent, 8 without
Queen (with 4″ separator bands) 78½″ × 85½″ (78½″ × 92″)	5	14	2	2 strips 9½″	14 strips 2½″	Cut 2½″ wide; 10 with accent, 10 without
	5	7	4	3 strips 9½″	11 strips 2½″	Cut 2½″ wide; 20 with accent, 20 without
King (with 4″ separator bands) 86″ × 85″ (86″ × 90″)	6	14	2	2 strips 8½″	14 strips 2½″	Cut 2½″ wide; 12 with accent, 12 without
	6	7	4	3 strips 8½″	11 strips 2½″	Cut 2½″ wide; 24 with accent, 24 without

Cutting—Triangles for Basic Braids; Separators for All Styles

Numbers are based on 40″ of useable width. All triangle strips are cut crosswise. All separators except crib size are cut lengthwise. See cutting configurations (below). Dimensions in parentheses are for braid variations. Wof = width of fabric, lof = length of fabric.

| Size without borders (w × l) | BASIC BRAID | | | | ALL STYLES | | |
	Starting triangles	Cutting configuration and number	Ending triangles —cut squares	Cutting configuration	Single separator	2-Fabric separator —outline strips	2-Fabric separator —center strips
Crib 27″ × 34″ (27″ × 38″)	5″ strip or 10″ square	cut 3—a or b	3 squares 5½″	c or d	2 strips 1½″–2½″ × wof	n/a	n/a
Lap 44″ × 62″ (44″ × 67″)	6½″ strip or 13″ square	cut 4—a or b	4 squares 7″	c or d	n/a	n/a	n/a
Twin 56″ × 73″ (56″ × 79″)	6½″ strip or 13″ square	cut 4—a or b	4 squares 7″	c or d	6 strips 4½″ × lof	12 strips 1½″ × lof	6 strips 2½″ × lof
Queen 78½″ × 85½″ (78½″ × 92″)	2 strips 7¼″ or 2 squares 14½″	cut 5—a or b	5 squares 7¾″	c	8 strips 4½″ × lof	16 strips 1½″ × lof	8 strips 2½″ × lof
King 86″ × 85″ (86″ × 90″)	2 strips 6½″ or 2 squares 13″	cut 6—a or b	6 squares 7″	c	5 strips 4½″ × lof	20 strips 1½″ × lof	10 strips 2½″ × lof

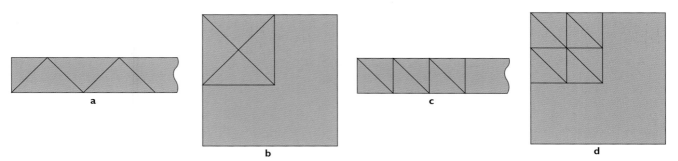

Cutting configurations; Drawings not to scale

Cutting—Center Squares and Triangles for Variations

Numbers are based on 40″ of useable width. All strips are cut crosswise. See cutting configurations (page 77).
FQ = fat quarter.

Size without borders (w × l)	CENTER-OUT			END-IN			
	Center squares	Ending triangles —cut squares	Cutting configuration	Starting triangles	Cutting configuration	Center triangles	Cutting configuration
Crib 27″ × 38″	3 squares 6⅜″	6 squares 5½″	c	1 strip 5″ or 2 strips 5″ from FQ or 2 squares 10″	cut 6— a or b	1 strip 5″ or 2 strips 5″ from FQ or 2 squares 10″	cut 6— a or b
Lap 44″ × 67″	4 squares 8⅜″	8 squares 7″	c	2 strips 6½″ or 4 strips 6½″ from FQs or 2 squares 13″	cut 8— a or b	2 strips 6½″ or 4 strips 6½″ from FQs or 2 squares 13″	cut 8— a or b
Twin 56″ × 78″	4 squares 8⅜″	8 squares 7″	c	2 strips 6½″ or 4 strips 6½″ from FQs or 2 squares 13″	cut 8— a or b	2 strips 6½″ or 4 strips 6½″ from FQs or 2 squares 13″	cut 8— a or b
Queen 78½″ × 92″	5 squares 9⅜″	10 squares 7¾″	c	3 strips 7¼″	cut 10—a	3 strips 7¼″	cut 10—a
King 86″ × 90″	6 squares 8″	12 squares 7″	c	3 strips 6½″	cut 12—a	3 strips 6½″	cut 12—a

Templates for *Mi Casa Es Su Casa* (page 45)

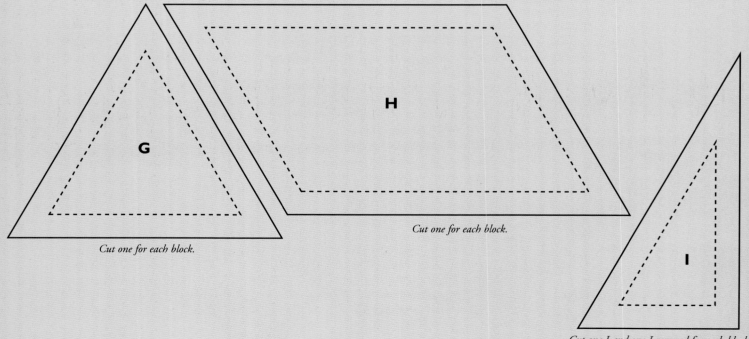

G

Cut one for each block.

H

Cut one for each block.

I

Cut one I and one I-reversed for each block.

About the Authors

Patricia Ritter

Jane Hardy Miller was born in and (mostly) grew up in California, where she attended college and law school. Her mother, a home economics teacher, taught her to sew by hand and machine beginning at age five. She made her first quilt in 1968, and for the following ten years made about one per year, inventing techniques as she went along. She practiced law briefly in Hawaii and California and then moved to Miami in 1979, where she married, had two children, and finally took a beginning quilting class. She has been working and teaching in a local quilt shop since 1987.

"Fabulous Florals" quilt pattern available at www.plumplesquiltpatterns.com

Arlene Netten, designer of "Fabulous Florals," the inspiration quilt design for this book, lives with her husband in Garden Valley, Idaho, a small mountain town one hour north of Boise; a perfect place to quilt, quilt, quilt! She immediately fell in love with quilting when she began in 1994 and her Plumples Quilt Patterns business soon followed. After a lifelong interest in sewing and crafts, she has found that quilting embodies the best of all the creative endeavors and, as a result, it has truly become her passion. Her other passion is her grandson, Ryan, who gives immeasurable joy!

Sources

For quilting supplies:
Cotton Patch Mail Order
3405 Hall Lane, Dept. CTB
Lafayette, CA 94549
(800) 835-4418 ▪ (925) 283-7883
Email: quiltusa@yahoo.com
Website: www.quiltusa.com

For a free catalog:
C&T Publishing, Inc.
P.O. Box 1456
Lafayette, CA 94549
(800) 284-1114
Email: ctinfo@ctpub.com
Website: www.ctpub.com

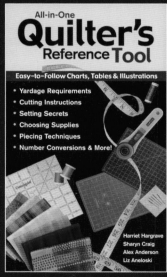
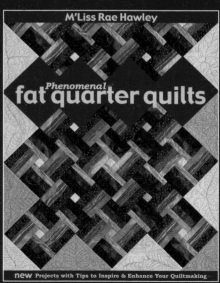